SYMBOLIC COMPUTATION

Artificial Intelligence

Springer Series
SYMBOLIC COMPUTATION - *Artificial Intelligence*

N.J. Nilsson: *Principles of Artificial Intelligence.* XV, 476 pages, 139 figs., 1982.

J.H. Siekmann, G. Wrightson (Eds.): *Automation of Reasoning 1. Classical Papers of Computational Logic 1957-1966.* XXII, 525 pages, 1983.

J.H. Siekmann, G. Wrightson (Eds.): *Automation of Reasoning 2. Classical Papers on Computational Logic 1967-1970.* XXII, 638 pages, 1983.

L. Bolc (Ed.): *The Design of Interpreters, Compilers, and Editors for Augmented Transition Networks.* XII, 214 pages, 72 figs., 1983.

R.S. Michalski, J.G. Carbonell, T.M. Mitchell (Eds.): *Machine Learning. An Artificial Intelligence Approach.* 572 pages, 1984.

L. Bolc (Ed.): *Natural Language Communication with Pictorial Information Systems.* VII, 327 pages, 67 figs., 1984.

A. Bundy (Ed.): *Catalogue of Artificial Intelligence Tools.* XXV, 150 pages, 1984. Second, revised edition, IV, 168 pages, 1986.

M.M. Botvinnik: *Computers in Chess. Solving Inexact Problems.* With contributions by A.I. Reznitsky, B.M. Stilman, M.A. Tsfasman, A.D. Yudin. Translated from the Russian by A.A. Brown. XIV, 518 pages, 48 figs., 1984.

C. Blume, W. Jakob: *Programming Languages for Industrial Robots.* XIII, 376 pages, 145 figs., 1986.

L. Bolc (Ed.): *Natural Language Parsing Systems.* XVII, 367 pages, 155 figs., 1987.

L. Bolc (Ed.): *Computational Models of Learning.* IX, 208 pages, 34 figs., 1987.

N. Cercone, G. McCalla (Eds.): *The Knowledge Frontier. Essays in the Representation of Knowledge.* XXXV, 522 pages, 93 figs., 1987.

G. Rayna: *REDUCE. Software for Algebraic Computation.* IX, 344 pages, 1987.

J.W. Lloyd: *Foundations of Logic Programming.* Second, Extended Edition. XII, 212 pages, 1987.

D. McDonald, L. Bolc (Eds.): *Natural Language Generation Systems.* XI, 400 pages, 84 figs., 1988.

continued after index

D. Navinchandra

Exploration and Innovation in Design
Towards a Computational Model

Foreword by John S. Gero

With 51 Illustrations

Springer-Verlag
New York Berlin Heidelberg London
Paris Tokyo Hong Kong Barcelona

D. Navinchandra
Robotics Institute
Carnegie Mellon University
Pittsburgh, Pennsylvania 15213
USA

Library of Congress Cataloging-in-Publication Data
Navinchandra, D.
    Exploration and innovation in design : towards a computational
model / D. Navinchandra.
        p.   cm. — (Symbolic computation. Artificial intelligence)
    Includes bibliographical references (p.   ) and index.
    1. Engineering design — Mathematical models.   2. Operations
research.   I. Title.   II. Series.
    TA174.N39   1991
    620'.0042 — dc20   90-19236

Printed on acid-free paper

Camera-ready copy provided by the author.
Printed and bound by R.R. Donnelley & Sons, Harrisonburg, Virginia.
Printed in the United States of America.

9 8 7 6 5 4 3 2 1

ISBN 0-387-97481-4 Springer-Verlag New York Berlin Heidelberg
ISBN 3-540-97481-4 Springer-Verlag Berlin Heidelberg New York

To my parents, Mrs. and Mr. Jithachandra, for making me study and for emphasizing the importance of education.

To my loving wife, Fatima, for encouraging me.

To Lord Sri. Venkateshwara.

I would like to thank *...

Mark Fox (Carnegie Mellon), for introducing me to the world of constraint directed systems, back in 1983. He got me interested in AI and its applications.

John Gero (Univ. of Sydney), for being very supportive of my design research from the very beginning. It was through my discussions with John that I first got interested in innovative design.

Mark Gross (Univ. of Colorado), for helping me develop an interest in constraint based design. For making many valuable suggestions to this book. For encouraging me when things were going slow.

Dr. Ravinder Jain (U.S. Army CERL), for his foresight in recognizing the importance of AI in engineering -- very early in the game.

M. Kim (Univ. of Illinois Urbana-Champaign), for helping me realize that design isn't just constraint satisfaction.

Robert Logcher (MIT), for inculcating in me a love of computers and computer-aided engineering - something that will stay with me for the rest of my life.

David H. Marks (MIT), for recognizing in me an aptitude for research. For suggesting and encouraging my investigations into design theory. For his personal warmth and caring. It is to him that I am most deeply grateful.

Ramesh Patil (USC), for helping me organize my thoughts and for providing valuable criticism. I appreciate the patience and care he put into reading and improving this book.

D. Sriram (MIT), for getting me excited about computer aided design. Many long discussions with Sriram helped me identify and pursue interesting research directions.

Dana Tomlin (Harvard, now at Ohio State), for helping me understand design and designers. It was he who told me about the role of criteria emergence in design. This idea is central to the thesis presented here.

---

*Alphabetically

Foreword

Design occupies a very special place in our society. Whether the designer is concerned with designing a building, a dam, an engine, a chemical process, a VLSI circuit, a social security system, or a software system, the resulting design will, in some sense, be different to any previously produced design. Designers are change agents within our society and they aim at improvement. As a result each design is expected to be better than the last and is therefore expected to be different.

Research into design is remarkably recent. Although researchers such as Durand at the Ecole Polytechnique in Paris published at the end of the eighteenth and early nineteenth centuries it was not until the development of computers and computable models of knowledge and knowledge representation that design research came into its own. Important influences came from systems theory, operations research, linguistics, artificial intelligence and cognitive science. All of these brought the notions of the scientific discipline to bear on design research. The term 'design science' was coined only in 1968 by Herbert Simon in his Karl Taylor Compton lectures at MIT.

Much of design research focuses on various aspects of routine design. This is clearly an important area and is the precursor for research into the area of non-routine design. The distinction between these two areas can be made by characterizing routine design as design where both the available decisions and the computational processes used to take those decisions are known prior to the commencement of a design. This is not to imply that routine design is in any sense trivial or even easy but rather to distinguish it from that class of design where the available decisions are not all known beforehand. Since designers in the search for the new, move outside the routine, research into non-routine design is necessary if we are to develop computational tools which will aid designers to be more creative. Such research has become the concern of many individuals and groups.

In one of the first books to present both conceptual and computational models of processes which have the potential to produce innovative results at the early stages of design, Navinchandra has made an important contribution. The fundamental concept espoused here is that of exploration where the system, using computational processes, moves outside the predefined available decisions. This is a requirement for innovative designs. I shall leave it to the reader to examine the ideas presented here and to understand and study the processes described and implemented. These processes, as brought together in this volume, further our understanding of computable models of design, particularly those that are capable of assisting in the production of non-routine designs. The ideas presented in this volume contribute to a vindication of Herbert Simon's 1968 statement that we are moving towards a 'science of design'.

John S. Gero
University of Sydney

Contents

Chapter 1
Introduction and Overview

Design is among the more complex tasks that humans perform. It is the process of producing artifacts that have desired properties and meet some functional requirements. Designing is a central skill in many human tasks: Architects deal with shape and form to create new buildings, financial planners manipulate money to design profitable portfolios, and mechanical engineers design functional machines with parts such as gears and cams.

Designers are constantly producing newer and better artifacts. In the modern competitive world, they are under constant pressure to turn out new and innovative products quickly. In order to improve the productivity of designers, computer aided design tools have been developed. In the short term, these efforts have focused primarily on automating the more routine and tedious tasks involved in design. Of the two major phases of a design process, *conceptual design* and *detailed design*, tool-building efforts have concentrated mainly on the latter phase. Applications have been limited to tasks such as computer-aided drafting, solid modeling, numerical optimization, simulation and analysis[1]. Having made substantial contributions towards the development of tools for detailed design, researchers are now focusing their attention on the earlier phase: conceptual design.

Conceptual design is that part of the design process in which: problems are identified, functions and specifications are laid out and appropriate solutions are generated through the combination of some basic building blocks. Conceptual design, unlike analysis, has no fixed procedure and involves a mix of numeric and symbolic reasoning. Research into

---

[1]Examples of such systems are: STRUDL (Structural Design Language [Roos 66]), SPICE (Electrical Network Analysis [SPICE2 75]) and GDS (a drafting tool [McDonnell Douglas 84]).

understanding and automating conceptual design has raised a set of issues very different from those governing the automation of design analysis and detailing.

Recently, researchers have started developing knowledge-based systems for conceptual design. The majority of these systems view design as a *search* process. For example, a system that designs buildings might search for solutions by trying various combinations of structural elements such as beams, columns, and slabs. One of the problems with using a search technique, however, is that if it is not properly controlled, it can easily lead to a combinatorial explosion. This problem has been addressed by using constraints and heuristics to guide the search [Fikes 69, Mackworth 77, Stefik 80, Fox 83]. These developments have served as the basis of several early efforts to automate conceptual design.

A majority of these efforts have concentrated on routine design problems. A design process is deemed routine if it involves a well understood sequence of steps where all decision points and outcomes are known *a priori* – there are no surprises. An advantage of developing systems for routine design is that, as the process is well understood, there is a rich set of design heuristics that can be used to effectively control the search. Routine design systems can be organized in several different ways. For example, (1) some routine design tasks can be broken into discrete steps, where each step performs some specific design sub-task; (2) in some cases, the problem can be approached hierarchically, where each level in the hierarchy is predetermined; and (3) in other cases, specific heuristics are available for different parts of the design. These heuristics can be packed into modules, where each module is responsible for one part of the overall design. Using strategies such as these, several systems have been built for various routine design applications. Examples of such applications: building design [Maher 84, Sriram 86], circuit design [Tong 88], and the design of mechanical devices [Mittal 85, Brown & Chandrasekaran 86, Steinberg et.al. 86].

Based on the success of the routine design systems, interest is now being generated in building systems that can handle non-routine design problems. Examples of such efforts are: (1) the EDISON project at UCLA which is aimed at building an invention system for mechanical devices [Dyer et.al. 86], (2) learning systems in architecture: abductive design rule learning for window-wall designs [McLaughlin and Gero 87] and chunking structural design knowledge [Gero et.al. 88], (3) structural element invention systems: the modification operator based PROMPT [Murthy & Addanki 87] and the first principles based

1stPRINCE [Cagan 88]. This is by no means a complete list of research efforts in non-routine design, an extensive survey may be found in [Navinchandra 90].

INNOVATIVE DESIGN

This book is about innovative conceptual design. The first question to ask is: What is Innovative Design? Simply put, something is innovative if it solves a known or a new problem in a way different from other known designs. The key to innovation, I believe, is being different. In this book we will examine what it means to be different, and how one goes about being different.

Unlike routine design approaches, innovative design systems have to work with far fewer guiding heuristics. Assumptions that could be made in the context of routine design cannot be used anymore. As there is no prior knowledge about the shape or structure of the solution to a problem, it is not possible to predetermine a set of steps that can be followed to produce a desired design. Second, the design criteria are liable to change during the design process. Criteria can either be relaxed or intensified, they can be deleted or new criteria can be brought into consideration. The decisions and tradeoffs to be made cannot be predetermined. Criteria and tradeoffs among them have to be handled dynamically – during the design process. Third, multiple design objectives may exist that have to be all maximized simultaneously. In non-routine design situations, there is no prior knowledge about the tradeoffs involved. There are only a handful of researchers who have worked on multi-objective optimization of conceptual designs [Wilde 78, Radford & Gero 86]. Fourth, in certain cases, a design may have problems that cannot be solved by searching only within the given solution space. The problem solver has to use information drawn from previous design experiences, in other words, the search has to be extended to Long Term Memory.

This book presents a computational model for conceptual design that addresses the issues listed above. We will show how some aspects of human innovative-design behavior can be mimicked by a computer program. The reader should note that it is not our aim to develop cognitive models of human thought, but to build practical computer tools that exhibit some characteristics of human approaches to innovative design. I don't claim that our computer programs reflect what is going on inside a designer's head; we are only trying to make the computer produce results that will appear innovative to an observer.

We will focus on two aspects of innovative design. First, on how designers *explore* many design alternatives before choosing a final one. We will examine why *exploration* plays an important role in innovative design. The second focus is on how designers apply past experiences (precedents) to solve design problems. It is by reasoning from precedents that designers are able to solve problems in interesting ways. This way of solving design problems is termed design *adaptation*.

In the rest of this introductory chapter we will examine a model of design and its relation to our central thesis. Following this, a description of our computational model of design is presented. Finally, a summary of the book is provided.

THE THESIS

There is no formula for design; the process draws upon a wide range of knowledge and problem-solving techniques. While no computer algorithm will ever replace designers, it is possible to develop tools that can help designers design. It is our *aim* to develop an architecture for a CAD tool which will help designers explore alternatives and adapt designs which have problems. We would like our system to automatically explore a large variety of design alternatives and report only the interesting ones to the user. In addition, we would like the system to help the designer adapt designs which have problems. Normally, a designer might adapt designs by reasoning from his experiences about previous design cases. We would like the system to aid the designer by suggesting adaptations drawn from a large database of past experiences. We hypothesize that a tool that can explore alternatives and adapt designs can help designers be more innovative.

Our thesis has three major parts. The first is that some useful design tasks can be modeled as configuration problems, and that search techniques can be used to find solutions to these problems. A configuration problem is defined as follows: Given a predefined set of primitive objects, find a way of arranging some or all of the objects such that the final arrangement (configuration) satisfies a given set of requirements (criteria). For example, a building is composed of primitives such as beams, columns, and slabs. It satisfies criteria regarding stability, economics, and access.

The second part of our thesis is that innovative designs can be obtained by exploring a wide variety of alternatives. Innovative designs are not obtained through some deliberate attempt at producing them, but by generating lots of design alternatives and throwing away the bad ones. Consequently, the ability of a system to innovate depends on how well it can generate diverse alternatives that break away from the norms and the governing constraints. We call this process *exploration*. An explorer deviates from the beaten path to generate unconventional solutions to problems. Explorers break away from the norms, relax constraints, and look in unlikely places. Exploration exposes possibilities that would not normally have been considered, possibilities which may serendipitously lead to innovative solutions.

The third part of our thesis is that one source of innovation, in a given design domain, comes from the ability to use knowledge drawn from sources inside or outside the current domain. In particular, a design will appear novel if it incorporates knowledge acquired from past experiences that come from sources that seem unrelated to the current design problem. For example, consider a person who is trying to design a new type of tent that deploys itself by snapping into place. As there are no existing tents that have this ability, the designer may not be able to solve the problem by using standard tent parts. She/He[2] will have to draw upon experiences from outside the domain of tent design. A device relevant to this problem is an umbrella. The designer can draw ideas from the umbrella to design his tent. The point is that some design problems *cannot* be solved if one is restricted to standard components and methods.

The use of non-standard precedents is key to innovative design because the perception of an artifact as being innovative lies, not in some inherent property of the artifact, *but in the eyes of the beholder*. For a given observer, or a given group of observers, there is a set of design styles they are accustomed to seeing in the artifacts designed by their peers. A construction equipment designer, for example, will view an excavation robot as being an innovation. A robot designer, on the other hand, will view the same robot as being just another application of familiar techniques. The robot's sophisticated vision, tactile and position sensing systems are not new to the robot designer and are part of the *design culture* he works within. For the construction engineer, conversely, an excavation robot is novel because robotics is outside his design culture.

A design culture is defined by the common practices, design styles and

---

[2]The designer is addressed as a "he" throughout the rest of this document, purely in the interest of fluid reading.

technologies used by people who operate within the culture. It defines the context they operate within, it's their weltanschauungen. Consequently, it is our thesis that innovation is based on the ability to reason from precedents taken from across design cultures. The notion of a design culture gives us a datum from which designs can be characterized, where, each design culture has its own way of viewing designs as being routine or innovative.

Spec.	Proc.	Prod.	Example
M	M	M	Structural beam design.
D	M	M	Where the application is novel but the solution is quite mundane. (e.g. office automation in a Church)
M	D	M	A new fast technique for designing structural beams.
M	M	D	Not Possible.
D	D	M	Similar to DMM, only this time a new technique leads to the same mundane solution.
M	D	D	A new method for solving an old problem. E.g. Use of VLSI chips to control a toaster oven.
D	M	D	A different spec. passes through a mundane process to produce a novel product. E.g. design a previously unknown circuit using known techniques.
D	D	D	A truly non-routine design situation.

LEGEND:
Spec.   Specifications to the design process.
Proc.   The design process.
Prod.   The product, the final design.
D   Different from the prevailing state in a design culture.
M   Mundane (Intra-Cultural Design)

Figure 1-1: Types of Design

Innovativeness is a relative notion. Where, the key is to be different from what is commonly known in a design culture. Refining this idea further, the "difference" of a design can be characterized along three dimensions: the initial *specification*, the design *process* and the final designed *product*. The table in Figure 1-1 shows eight ways in which a design can be different. The characterization uses a coarse metric of difference. The design specifications, the design process or the design itself can be either *mundane* or *different* with respect to a given design culture. Something is mundane if it is part of the culture and is known to those who belong to the design culture. The table goes to show that there is no objective demarcation between routine and innovative design, but rather a continuum ranging from purely routine to innovative.

In Figure 1-1, the word "different" is used to denote that a particular aspect (specification, product, or process) is unlike the norms of the given design culture. The word is used loosely. In reality, there are several shades of difference between a design and the design culture it is part of. Let's examine this aspect even further.

Shades of Difference

To an observer based in a design culture, a given design will appear different if it either borrows ideas from other cultures or is a new combination of ideas already familiar to the observer. It may appear that our definition of difference assumes that a designer (the observer) operates from within one culture only. In fact, the definition is extendible to observers who are at the intersection of many cultures. For example, for an electro-mechanical machine designer, only ideas from outside both the electrical and mechanical engineering domains will qualify as extra-cultural.

Generalizing this idea further, we believe that the definition applies to any observer who is aware of a very large variety of cultures, including domains that have no direct bearing on design. For example, a mechanical engineer works with ideas from within the mechanical domain and from related areas such as electronics, sensor technology, and materials. While designing, though aware of a wide variety of disciplines (e.g. art, housework, cooking, sports etc.), the designer brings to bear knowledge drawn from a few main and some related cultures relevant to the task at hand.

If a designer reaches for new ideas beyond the knowledge he normally uses during design, his product will appear different. The further he reaches, the more different or novel his design will appear. The reason for this phenomenon is that, for a given culture, there are some cultures (or domains) that are perceived as being related while other cultures are viewed as being far and unrelated. When ideas are transferred between unrelated cultures then design solutions appear different, perhaps novel. The relatedness, or un-relatedness of cultures is determined socially, and is constantly in flux. For example, when ideas about automation were first taken from industrial assembly lines to applications at home (washers, food processors) the transfer was considered very novel. In fact, companies had problems trying to convince homemakers that automation at home is safe and acceptable. Today, advanced electronics is viewed as part of the home appliance design culture. We are now accustomed to programmable ovens and talking refrigerators.

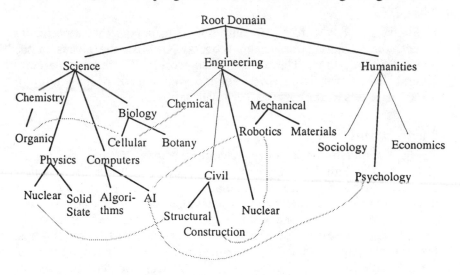

Figure 1-2: A Domain Hierarchy

The "novelty" of a new design composed of two or more ideas taken from different domains can be measured using a hierarchical classification of domains. This approach works well in a computer. The tree shown in Figure 1-2 shows relationships among domains as an acyclic graph. Cross connections among domains is shown by grey lines. In this framework, the larger the number of arcs one has to traverse to go from one domain to another, the more different (or distant) they are. As more and more novel designs are generated, the hierarchical structure has to be reorganized to reflect which domains are regarded as being close and which ones continue to be unrelated. Such domain graphs are particularly useful in innovative design systems. For example, if one has to choose among two competing extra-cultural strategies for debugging a design, choosing the strategy taken from a more distant domain will make the final solution appear innovative. There are merits and demerits of this approach. On the minus side, ideas drawn from farther cultures are more likely to fail. On the plus side, a novel solution may serendipitously solve the problem or may satisfy a wider set of criteria than originally anticipated.

In this section we have seen how innovative design behavior can be achieved by being different, and how the differences can lie in the design specifications, process or final product. We also examined a means for measuring differences. But being different, though central to our theory of innovation, is not sufficient for innovative design. Every design that is different is not going to be innovative. As stated earlier, innovation can be achieved through exploration: that is, by generating a wide variety of designs and throwing away the bad ones. Achieving variety among alternatives is the most important aspect of exploration. Producing lots of very similar alternatives is not fruitful. Alternatives should be different, culturally far apart, and cross-cultural in nature. The generation of such alternatives can be viewed as a search process being conducted within and across design cultures.

Design Cultures as Search Spaces

The notion of a design culture gives us a datum from which designs can be characterized, where, each culture has its own way of viewing designs as being either routine or innovative. Designers working within a culture produce solutions to new problems by using known techniques to combine known technologies. For example, a building designer might work with floor slabs, pillars and walls which are part of the physical *technology* of the culture. The building design is developed by shaping and composing the available physical parts and materials using standard practices, styles and methods (*technique*). For instance, the creation of bays with regularly spaced pillars and the creation of rooms by erecting walls between pillars.

Designs that are based on known compositions of techniques (practices and styles) from within a culture will appear mundane. The corresponding design task is one of puzzle solving [Kuhn 70]. Even if individual mundane solutions may be different from one another they will only be part of current practice.

There are many ways in which a design can deviate from the mundane. These ideas are best explained using the notion of a search space. The aim of developing such an explanation is to characterize and specify ways for achieving variety. Consider the problem spaces shown in Figure 1-3. The outermost region (A-space) is the space of all legal combinations of the technology base available in a culture. For

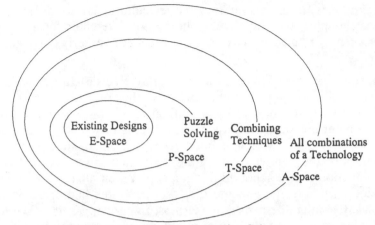

Figure 1-3: State Spaces of a Design Culture

example, in electronic chip design, all possible layouts of logic gates make up the A-space of the culture. Note that only legal combinations are allowed, as defined by basic physical laws. For example, two gates cannot occupy the same space. At the core of the A-space is the space of existing designs (E-space). Surrounding the core is the space of all designs that could be developed using the currently known heuristics, patterns and styles. This is the space generated by Puzzle Solving (P-space). During puzzle-solving, the designer is only responding to new situations using known techniques and technologies. The P-space can be extended by trying new combinations of known techniques. Designs generated in this way are said to be in the T-space

Let's consider an example from the domain of recipe design. A recipe generally has two parts: a list of ingredients (technology) and a method of preparation (technique). One can imagine coming up with a new dish by using the ingredients of one recipe, but using a method that combines the methods of two or more recipes. For instance, one could imagine combining a cake and a cookie recipe. Using the ingredients for a cake, one could use a combination of techniques taken from the cake and cookie recipes. This will probably produce little cakes which are crispy outside but soft and fluffy inside.

Finally, a design (or part thereof) may be generated by randomly permuting available technologies. This process can generate designs which known techniques cannot. Permuting elements of a design culture's technology can generate solutions anywhere in the A-space of the culture.

In this framework, any design solution outside the P-space will appear different from the norm and can potentially be an innovation. The question is, how does one explore beyond the P-space? What approaches and/or algorithms should one use?

AN APPROACH TO INNOVATIVE DESIGN

The key to innovation by exploration is achieving variety in the alternatives generated. A good exploration algorithm is sufficient to develop an innovative design system with. The problem, however, is efficiency. There is a direct tradeoff between exploration and normal problem solving (puzzle solving). Consider, for example, a design system that uses tree search to find solutions that satisfy specified constraints. Such a system might use a process of (a) branching, (b) constraint propagation, (c) pruning, (d) selection and re-branching till a feasible solution is found. Such problem solvers are designed to find solutions quickly, that is, by eliminating unlikely branches early on. Exploration, on the other hand, tries not to prune away branches even if constraints are violated. An explorer generates alternatives for the sake of generating them. The aim is to not miss an alternative which may: (a) serendipitously solve the given problem, (b) remind the problem solver of some other design or past experience that may contribute to the current solution, (c) remind the problem solver or design agent of a new criterion which may be relevant to the current context. Such occurrences can dramatically change the nature of the given design problem and the final product. An innovative design system, consequently, has to be able to generate a variety of alternatives and examine them to recognize interesting combinations and/or solutions. This corresponds to the basic Generate and Test idea [Feigenbaum 71]. We extend this by adding a debugging step [Navinchandra 87][3]. Our approach to innovative design has three parts:

1. Exploration

2. Evaluation

3. Adaptation

In the course of this book, we will examine computer based approaches to the *explore-evaluate-adapt* paradigm. The ideas and algorithms we examine will be in the context of a computer program called

---

[3]A similar notion was independently suggested by Simmons [Simmons 88].

CYCLOPS[4] that implements the ideas listed above. CYCLOPS operates in three primary modes: the *normal search* mode, the *exploration* mode and the *adaptation* mode.

1. In the *normal search* mode, the program performs a tree like search of design alternatives. It uses given design criteria to guide the search by pruning sub-optimal solutions. Left to itself, the normal search mode will eventually produce designs that satisfy all the given criteria, provided such solutions exist.

2. In the *exploration* mode, CYCLOPS relaxes the governing criteria and searches alternatives outside the original space of solutions. There are two reasons why we would like our system to relax criteria: (1) In some situations, the normal search mode is unable to find solutions. This happens when the problem is over-constrained. (2) The second reason is based on our finding that criteria relaxation is useful, not only in over-constrained problems, but also where solutions to the design problem are readily available. This is because criteria relaxation could find a design alternative which, by accident, turns out to be better than the ones available. There are two reasons, in turn, why this happens: (a) The solution space tends to be non-continuous, non-convex, and non-monotonic. Due to the fragmented nature of the space it is possible that a relaxation might expose unseen peaks in the design space. (b) The second reason why a new alternative can, unexpectedly, turn out to be better than other known alternatives is serendipity. During exploration, the system sometimes finds alternatives which provide opportunities that are not part of the original set of design criteria. The program recognizes opportunities by matching new designs to prior experiences (precedents). If a new alternative is found to be similar to a precedent in the database, the precedent is retrieved and used. When this happens, we say that the program has been *reminded* of a past experience. If the retrieved precedent satisfies some criterion not present in the current design problem, then the criterion is added to the current design problem. In this way, the system increases the value of a design alternative by adding a new factor to the evaluation. It is in this way that CYCLOPS discovers opportunities. Consider the following scenario:

> A landscape designer is working on the layout of suburban neighborhoods. Using constraints about acceptable slopes, soil conditions, aspect, etc., he delineates suitable regions of the landscape. He then starts locating various housing units on suitable

---

[4]Criteria Yielding, Consistent Labeling, Optimization and Precedents-based System

sites. After completing a preliminary layout he sits back to inspect his work. He now considers exploring more alternatives before making a final commitment. He decides to slightly relax a constraint on maximum allowable slope, and starts examining locations that had initially been eliminated by the constraint. While doing this, he suddenly finds a location which provides a view similar to the picturesque view of a house he had worked on previously. He had overlooked this location because it was too steep and had been eliminated by the slope constraint. He now introduces "view" as a new criterion for all sites and redesigns the layout.

3. In the *adaptation* mode, CYCLOPS uses precedent knowledge to adapt faulty designs. Defects can be introduced in a design during synthesis, criteria emergence or criteria relaxation. For example, if the program finds an interesting solution by relaxing criteria in the exploration mode, it will have to find some way of compensating for the relaxation. In the landscape design scenario, above, we saw how a designer relaxed a constraint and found an opportunity. There is, however, a price to pay – the new site is very steep. The designer will have to find an adaptation. A good place to find adaptations is in previous designs where *similar* situations were encountered. We have found that drawing strategies from past cases is an effective way to debug designs [Navinchandra 88]. Cases provide memories of past failures and solutions, which can be used to warn the problem solver of impending problems and to repair failures without having to work from scratch [Hammond 86, Kolodner 87]. We have observed that cases which are analogically related to the design problem can contribute repair strategies which would not normally have been generated by the system's existing heuristics.

When CYCLOPS is given the problem of dealing with a steep site, it looks through its database of precedents and finds a case in which terracing is used for hillside farming. Using this precedent, it attempts to terrace the site for the housing units. The program finds and uses the precedent case by drawing an analogy between mountain farming practices and its house location problem. Using analogies[5] for problem solving is a very effective way of extracting and using knowledge in cases which, at first glance, may not appear to be relevant to the problem at hand. Details on CYCLOPS' similarity determination techniques will be discussed in Chapter 6.

---

[5]A lot of work has been done on understanding analogies [Evans 68, Tversky 77, Winston 80, Carbonell 86, Kedar-Cabelli 85a]. An overview of analogy may be found in [Kedar-Cabelli 85b] and an overview of applications to design may be found in [Navinchandra 90].

Architecture of CYCLOPS

The CYCLOPS program has several modules and its architecture can be viewed in layers. At the heart of the system is the basic search process which consists of a synthesis module (*synthesizer*) and a selection module (*selector*). The synthesizer takes a set of partial solutions as input and adds detail to them. For example, a synthesizer might take a partial layout and add a few more houses to it. The designs produced by the synthesizer are tested by a selector (Figure 1-4, Part I). The selector uses the given design criteria to select partial designs for further detailing. If, at any stage, a complete design passes selection, it is output as a solution. This cycle is the normal-search process that CYCLOPS performs. If CYCLOPS is unable to find a solution using this process or, if the user decides to examine alternatives beyond the normal solution space, the program enters the exploration mode.

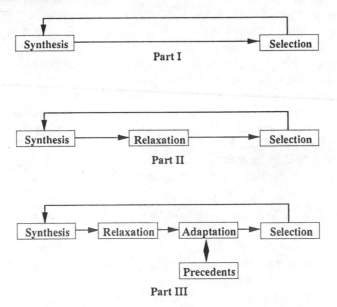

Figure 1-4: Architecture of CYCLOPS

CYCLOPS is able to explore alternatives by using a *relaxation* module (Figure 1-4, Part II). In this module, the governing criteria are relaxed to allow more partial solutions to pass selection than normally would have.

Finally, CYCLOPS has a precedent database it can draw upon (Figure 1-4, Part III). These precedents are used in two ways: First, the precedents are used as a source of new criteria. When the synthesis and relaxation modules produce alternatives, they are checked by the precedents. If a precedent finds a problem or an opportunity, a corresponding criterion is added to the selector. Secondly, precedents are used to patch problems in design alternatives. This step is called *adaptation* and is done by reasoning either directly or analogically from precedent cases.

ORGANIZATION OF THE BOOK

The ideas presented in the book are centered around one extended example, a design scenario presented in Chapter 2. Reading the scenario chapter should give the reader a complete, intuitive picture of the approach. The rest of the book addresses our three major theses. Chapters 3 and 4 are about design representation and search. Chapter 5 discusses design exploration and the emergence of new criteria. Chapter 6 is about precedent based adaptation. Chapter 7 presents the overall architecture and shows how all the pieces fit together into one coherent system. The book ends with two concluding chapters. The first of which (Chapter 8) presents relationships to other research efforts. The last chapter (Chapter 9) discusses applications and future directions.

The following paragraphs present the major ideas in a summary form, using terminology taken from the design, artificial intelligence and operations research literatures. The complete chapters will provide a proper introduction (wherever possible) to the terms used. The reader may choose to skip the rest of this chapter and move on to the scenario.

Chapter 2: A Design Scenario

Scenario. A landscape design scenario is presented in detail.

Chapter 3: The Design Problem

Representing the design. The representation of configuration type designs is examined. A design is said to be configured if it is a combination of primitive objects. A configuration design is represented by a configuration language which is simply a collection of statements about objects and their inter-relationships. The design representation used here is called *local labeling*. The labeling problem is represented as a set of variables. Each variable has associated with it, a set of values from which one value may be chosen and assigned to the variable. A set of assignments that covers all the variables constitutes a complete configuration.

Chapter 4: Design Synthesis

Design Criteria. Acceptable designs are characterized by criteria, which can come in two forms: constraints and objectives. It is required that the final design simultaneously satisfy the given set of constraints. Further, the final design should be optimal with respect to the given objectives.

Selection by Optimality. Because design problems often involve many complex and often conflicting objectives, the solution process should be able to handle such complexity. Our solution technique is based on the traditional A^* search algorithm. The algorithm has been extended to handle multiple objectives. This is done by using pareto optimality to evaluate partial designs in the search tree. The modified algorithm is called *Pareto Optimality* based A^*.

Criteria Relaxation. As design is a criteria satisfaction process, it is the aim of the designer to attain the "best" design possible. It is, however, not always possible to find a design that simultaneously satisfies all the constraints and is optimal with respect to all the objectives. Designers often find themselves dealing with over-constrained, sub-optimal situations. Under these conditions, the designer has to relax constraints and tradeoff among the objectives in order to find a solution. We will develop an unified technique for handling both mechanisms. The technique is called criteria relaxation, where, a criterion is any proposition about design, be it a constraint or an objective. Making a tradeoff in any multi-criteria situation is a difficult decision for the designer. There is a vast literature concentrating in this area. Issues relating to utility theory, value assessments and tradeoff analysis is outside the scope of this book.

Chapter 5: Design Exploration

Design Exploration. Designing goes beyond the mere satisfaction of criteria. Designers like to explore alternatives and be adventurous while solving hard design problems. If a designer is presented with a design that satisfies all the criteria, it is possible that he may not be fully satisfied with it. He may still want to explore new designs in an attempt to find something interesting. In the model presented, exploration is done by relaxing the expected utility on each criteria. When we relax criteria, we are prepared to accept designs that would normally have been pruned off the search tree. These alternatives, through a synthesis process, go on to produce new designs.

Criteria Emergence. The criteria imposed on a design problem are always subject to change. While exploring alternatives, a designer may come across a situation that may influence him to change the original set of criteria, add new criteria or relax old ones. The designer continually recognizes problems and opportunities in his design, drawing upon a knowledge base of precedents. All criteria, prior or emergent, come from this knowledge base.

A technique for representing precedents is proposed. A precedent represents some past experience. We use a frame-based [Minsky 75] data structure with slots for:

- the **conditions** of the experience;
- the **effects** of the experience, which may be either emotional or physical;
- an **explanation** of how the effects followed from the conditions.

Whenever exploration unearths new design alternatives, new criteria may emerge. This process can often change the course of the design process.

Chapter 6: Design Adaptation

Design Adaptation. When a design alternative runs into problems, they can sometimes be solved by reasoning from previously acquired precedents. A precedent-based problem solving technique, called **demand posting** is presented. The process of resolving design problems starts with posting a demand on the database of precedents. If a precedent is found, it is applied. If not, the problem's causal explanation is retrieved and posted. This process continues recursively till an appropriate precedent is found. If all fails, the demand is posted to the user.

Chapters 7, 8, 9.

Overview, related research, and future directions.

Appendix A.

Formal Treatment of CLOP. A formal treatment of the Consistent Labeling Optimization Problem. The appendix presents the Pareto-Optimality based A^* algorithm with a proof of its admissibility.

Appendix B.

A Trace of CYCLOPS in action. A trace of one of the implementations of CYCLOPS is provided. The different modules in CYCLOPS are described.

SUMMARY:

Thesis	Techniques	Chapters
Design as a multi-criteria configuration problem.	Modified A* algorithm for multiple criteria.	Chapters 3 and 4
Design innovation through exploration.	Exploration through criteria relaxation and the emergence of new criteria.	Chapter 5
Design innovation through precedent-based reasoning.	Analogical Reasoning used for design adaptation.	Chapter 6

Chapter 2
A Design Scenario

In this chapter a hypothetical scenario, taken from the domain of landscape design, traces the steps that might be taken by a machine problem solver as it goes about solving a design problem[6]. Interspersed with this is an account of how a computer program could be implemented to take similar design steps.

Our example will let us examine how search techniques may be used to find optimal solutions in multi-objective design situations. The scenario shows how new designs may be explored by relaxing constraints and by making tradeoffs among objectives. During exploration, we will see how new criteria can sometimes emerge – leading to the discovery of opportunities or to the recognition of unexpected problems. Finally, we will see how previous design cases can be used to solve problems in interesting ways.

THE PROBLEM

Consider the following design problem: A region in the south-west section of town is to be developed. Eight lots of land are available for purchase and subsequent development. Five landuses; namely, a *recreational-area*, an *apartment-complex*, a cluster of 50 *single family houses*, a large *dumpsite*, and a *cemetery* are to be sited in this region.

Assume that the characteristics of the site have been determined using a standard geographic mapping system. A map of the site is shown in figure 2-1. The map shows eight lots of land which are available for development.

---

[6]Disclaimer: In places, the scenario tends to anthropomorphize the problem solver. This is done only to make the examples more intuitive, I am not claiming that the computer program is sentient in any way.

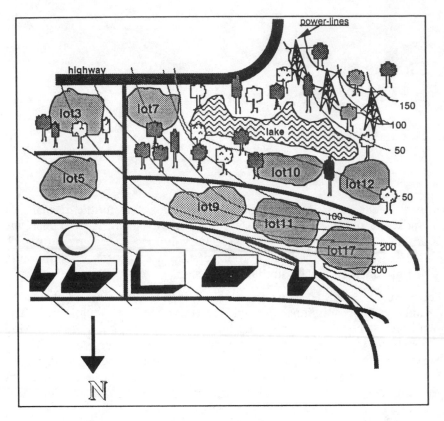

Figure 2-1: The site

Lot3, lot5, lot7 and lot9 are all relatively flat sites with fairly good soil conditions. Lot10 and lot12 are moderately sloped sites in a nice wooded location, but have poor soil conditions. Lot11 is a steep site with good soil conditions. Lot17 is a very steep site. Lot11 and lot17 are elevated sites facing southwest and down into a valley that has a lake and some wooded area.

The problem solver's task is to come up with assignments of landuses to sites. A complete design is one in which each landuse has been assigned to a lot. The final design should be one which complies with a given set of criteria:

1. **The Dumpsite and the cemetery should not be visible from either of the dwellings (i.e. houses or apartments).**

2. **The recreational area should be near some body of water.**

3. **Steep slopes are to be avoided for building.**

4. **Poor soil should be avoided for those landuses that involve construction.**

5. **The highway is noisy and ugly and should be avoided when locating the apartments, the single-family housing complex and the recreational areas.**

Based on these criteria, the problem solver then prepares a table (Figure 2-2), showing the compatibility of each of the proposed landuses with respect to the different available lots of land. In the table, criteria 2,3,4 and 5 have been depicted. It is not possible to represent criterion 1 in this way. This is because it is a relationship between two landuses that have not been sited as yet. Such criteria are said to be binary (i.e., they relate two sitable objects). Binary criteria may also be represented as tables, but separately from the other unary criteria. The table in Figure 2-3 tabulates all possible combinations of locations for the dumpsite and the housing complex. Xs are marked where criterion 1 is violated, and **OK**s are marked where the criterion is satisfied. A similar table could be prepared for the apartment buildings.

Landuse	lot3	lot5	lot7	lot9	lot10	lot11	lot12	lot17
Recreat-ional	no lake	no lake	OK	no lake	OK	no lake	OK	no lake
Apartment-complex	high-way too close	OK	high-way too close	OK	poor soil	steep	poor soil	very steep
Housing-sector	high-way too close	OK	high-way too close	OK	poor soil	steep	poor soil	very steep
Dumpsite	OK	OK	OK	OK	OK	steep	OK	very steep
Cemetery	OK	OK	OK	OK	OK	steep	OK	very steep

Figure 2-2: Tabular representation of the unary constraints

		3	5	7	9	10	11	12	17
H	3	X	OK	X	OK	OK	OK	OK	OK
o	5		X	X	X	OK	OK	OK	OK
u	7			X	OK	OK	OK	OK	OK
s	9				X	OK	X	OK	OK
i	10					X	X	X	X
n	11						X	X	X
g	12							X	X
	17								X

Figure 2-3: Binary Criterion: Dumpsite should not be visible from the housing complex.

A Solution is found

Assume that the problem solver comes up with the following assignments: cemetery at lot3, housing-sector at lot5, dumpsite at lot7, apartment-complex at lot9, and the recreation-area at lot10. This design has several interesting ideas. The dumpsite and the cemetery which are relatively noise insensitive, are placed next to the noisy highway. The problem solver also has ensured that neither the dumpsite nor the cemetery can be seen from the dwellings. This is because the apartment complex is placed on Lot9 and not on Lot5[7]. As the apartment complex is a high rise building, it is placed farther from Lot3 and Lot7. The single family housing complex, being a group of low rise buildings, will not be able to view the cemetery, even though it's close by; the trees in between lot3 and lot5 will block the view. The recreational area is near a lake and is sufficiently far from the dumpsite. This is an acceptable design as it satisfies the given criteria.

Two approaches could be used to develop a satisfactory design like the one just described. The first approach involves reasoning about the problem deductively. A deductive process might proceed something like this: *"The apartment complex is a high rise structure and hence*

---

[7]According to the Table in Figure 2-2, these are the only sites available to the two dwellings.

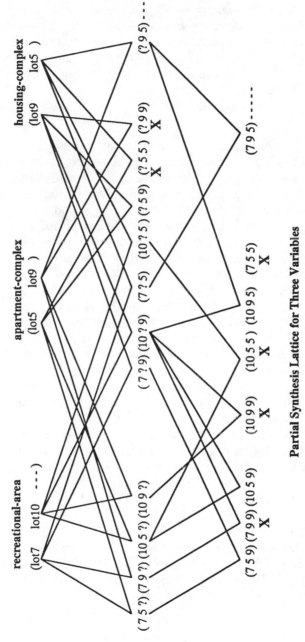

Partial Synthesis Lattice for Three Variables

Figure 2-4: Partial synthesis of the example design problem.

*has a far reaching view, it should be far from the dumpsite and the
cemetery. The single-family housing is a low rise building and could
be placed next to the cemetery but not the dumpsite. That's because the
cemetery has trees around it and the dumpsite is noxious. The lots near
the highway are noisy and could accommodate noise insensitive
landuses..."* This is a technique that people might use to solve the
problem. If the problem had 50 landuses and over a 100 sites, this
method would obviously not be practical and could drive anybody
bananas!

The second approach follows a different philosophy. Instead of
thinking through deductively, a systematic search could be used. The
idea is to generate partial designs and to discard those which are
inconsistent with the given criteria. For a given partial design, one does
not spend time thinking about all the criteria and strategies for the
placement of landuses; one just checks the design for consistency. If
inconsistencies are found, then the partial design is discarded. An
example of the search process is shown in Figure 2-4. The figure
shows three landuses (variables) being synthesized. The synthesis is
done in stages, where detail is added in each stage. The synthesis is
started by listing the possible values each variable can take. The three
variables: recreational-area, apartment-complex and housing-sector,
are listed with their corresponding set of possible assignments. For
example, the recreational-area can be located at either of lot7, lot10 or
lot12 (the other choices have been dropped in order to keep the figure
simple). In the first stage of synthesis the values of the variables are
combined into pairs. For example, the leftmost solution of the first
stage of the synthesis has the recreational-area on lot7 and the
apartment-complex on lot5, and as this is only the first stage of
synthesis, the solution has no information on where the housing-sector
will be sited. The solution is denoted as (7 5 ?), where "?" stands for
the location of the third variable, the housing complex. At the end of
each stage of synthesis, all the generated solutions are evaluated against
the given criteria; overlapping choices are Xed out. Violating solutions
are discarded before proceeding. At the next stage of the synthesis, the
partial solutions are paired into complete solutions. For example, the
leftmost solution in the second stage: (7 5 9) is formed by joining (7 5
?) and (7 ? 9). This systematic exploration of alternatives is amenable
to computerization.

Adding some objectives

Let us now return to the landscape design scenario, and add two new criteria:

6. The cost of acquired land should be minimized.

7. The total of excess noise for all the landuses should be minimized.

Solving the design problem now involves satisfying criteria 1 thru 5 and simultaneously optimizing criteria 6 and 7. This requires the calculation of total cost and total noise levels. Let's assume that the cost (in millions) and noise levels (in Noise Factors) for the sites are as follows:

Lot	Cost	NF
Lot3	$1.2 M	45 NF
Lot5	$1.3 M	30 NF
Lot7	$0.9 M	37 NF
Lot9	$1.6 M	20 NF
Lot10	$1.7 M	22 NF
Lot11	$1.0 M	20 NF
Lot17	$0.8 M	20 NF
Lot12	$1.4 M	22 NF

The total cost is simply the sum of the costs of the plots of land. The total noise is the sum of the excess noise at each site. The excess noise at a site is found by comparing the site's noise with the acceptable NF level of the landuse sited there. The total excess noise is called the Effective Noise Factor[8] (ENF). The acceptable NF for the different landuses are: recreational-area, 20NF; apartment-complex, 30NF; housing-complex, 25NF; dumpsite, 50NF; and cemetery, 35NF.

We now have a multi-objective optimization problem at hand. The

---

[8]The author would like to remind the reader that this is only a scenario. The actual techniques used for calculating cost and noise are not important. Do not stop to verify calculations, the purpose of this chapter is to provide the reader an intuitive grasp of the process.

difficulty with multi-objective problems is that the objectives are often at odds. In our example, the cost minimization objective would prefer the cheaper lots: lot11, lot17 and lot7. On the other hand, the noise minimization objective will avoid lot7. Of the cheaper lots remaining, both lot11 and lot17 happen to exceed the maximum allowable slope constraint. In real problems we may have dozens of such objectives, all interacting with one another.

	Recr-ation	Apart ments	Hous-ing	Dump site	Ceme tery	Cost	ENF
Noise-Levels	20	30	25	50	35		
Alter-natives:							
A	lot10	lot5	lot9	lot7	lot3	6.7	14
B	lot7	lot9	lot5	lot12	lot3	6.4	32
C	lot12	lot5	lot9	lot7	lot10	7.1	4
D	lot10	lot12	lot7	lot5	lot3	6.5	24
E	lot10	lot7	lot12	lot3	lot5	6.5	9

Figure 2-5: A set of design configurations, their costs and ENF

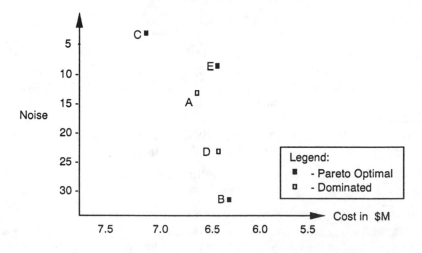

Figure 2-6: Pareto curve for cost vs noise.

Under these conditions, the solution to the design problem involves tradeoffs among the objectives. A simple and intuitive way of handling tradeoffs is to plot the different partial designs onto a graph. For example, consider a set of alternate design configurations (A through E) shown in Figure 2-5. The cost and noise factors for the alternatives can be plotted on a graph of noise vs. cost (Figure 2-6). In the graph, solutions A and D are inferior to E. The solutions B, C and E are not inferior to any other known solution. These solutions are said to be *pareto optimal* [Pareto 96]. A particular solution is said to be pareto optimal if it is not dominated by any other solution, that is, if no other solution improves upon it with respect to all the given objectives (dimensions of the graph). Conversely, a solution X is said to be dominated if there is any other solution Y (which does not overlap X) on the graph, such that, X does not have better values than Y with respect to **any** of the given objectives (dimensions of the graph). This definition of pareto optimality gives us a method of dividing a set of solutions into two groups: the dominated set and the non-dominated (Pareto Optimal) set.

Evaluating partial designs

In the example above, we saw how a given set of design alternatives may be evaluated using pareto-optimality conditions. This approach, however, is not appropriate for large problems. In order to apply the technique, completed designs must be generated first and then tested for optimality. Substantial savings in computation may be achieved by moving the evaluation up into the generation phase, allowing us to discard bad designs long before they are completed. This approach may be viewed as a continuous synthesis process, in which, designs are evaluated at the end of each synthesis step, and only the optimal partial designs are allowed to enter every new stage of synthesis.

The synthesis-pruning process presented above, however, is not guaranteed to produce optimal solutions. By pruning off a partial design early in the synthesis process, it is possible to inadvertently cut off a branch leading to an optimal solution. To prevent his from happening, the search can be ordered in such a way that more attractive alternatives are considered first. If any of these alternatives, upon further examination, are not found to be optimal, then the algorithm returns to previously discarded solutions. This technique is called Best-First Search [Nilsson 80].

To implement Best-First search, we need some method for evaluating partial designs. In our example, optimality is determined by calculating the total cost and total noise factor (ENF) of designs. But this raises the question: How can we calculate the total cost of a design that is only partially complete? Although we can calculate the cost of whatever has been designed so far, we cannot find the total cost until the design is complete. It is possible, however, to *estimate* the cost of completing the partial design.

For example, consider a partial design in which we have selected lot3 for the dump, lot5 for the cemetery and lot9 for the housing complex, and we have yet to locate the apartment-complex and the recreational-area. In this case, the best way to estimate the cost of the last two landuses is to make an estimate of the final cost. From Figure 2-2 (page 21), we can see that the recreational area can be sited on either lot7 ($0.9m) or lot10 ($1.7m) or lot12 ($1.4m) and the apartment complex can be sited on lot5 ($1.3m) or lot9 ($1.6m). In order to estimate the cost of the yet-to-be-sited landuses one may optimistically assume that the landuses will be assigned to the cheapest of the remaining possible locations. In the example, let's assume that the recreational area gets assigned to lot7 ($0.9m) and the apartment complex gets assigned to lot5 ($1.3m). The most optimistic estimate of the cost for the completion of the design is, hence, $2.2m.

The estimate is optimistic because it disregards other criteria that might prevent the design from taking the best possible configuration. By choosing the best possible locations for the remaining landuses, the estimate, though inaccurate, is optimistic. Interestingly, the use of optimistic estimates for searching the design space is guaranteed to yield optimal solutions. This notion, in the artificial intelligence literature, is called A^* search [Nilsson 80]. Details on how these ideas apply to design are presented later in the book.

The use of search techniques, however sophisticated, cannot help us actually choose among pareto optimal designs. For example, in figure 2-6 solutions B, E and C are all optimal along some dimension. Choosing one of these designs involves making a tradeoff which prefers one dimension over the other. This book does not examine the utility and preference structures that underlie such decisions. It is left to the user to choose among equally good (pareto-optimal) design alternatives. If the user cannot choose, he can just indicate that he is indifferent among the different pareto optimal solutions. The user has the last word, since there always will be many subjective criteria that cannot be expressed quantitatively or symbolically, even in the context of the narrow domain chosen.

Many techniques have been developed for handling tradeoffs among multiple objectives [Haimes etal. 75, Chankong & Haimes 83, Zionts

77, Zionts & Wallenius 80, Goicoechea 82]. A problem with these techniques is that they can only handle tradeoffs among objectives. The question is, if we can relax the objectives to find answers, why don't we relax the constraints too? One of the central hypotheses of our research is that constraint relaxation coupled with objective relaxation plays an important role in design. Let's examine why.

DESIGN EXPLORATION

In Figure 2-6, designs B, C and E are non-dominated. The problem solver can choose the final design from among these alternatives. If, however, the problem solver wishes to find better solutions it could do so by exploring new alternatives – perhaps by relaxing the governing criteria. In our scenario, let us assume the problem solver decides to relax the slope constraint. In Figure 2-2 (Page 21), lot11 and lot17 were discarded because of steep slopes. As lot17 is steeper than lot11, a marginal relaxation of the slope constraint will bring only lot11 into consideration. Two new designs F and G are now generated. These new designs are added to the graph shown in Figure 2-6. The new graph is shown in Figure 2-7. The configurations of F and G are shown below:

	Recr-ation	Apart-ments	Hous-ing	Dump site	Ceme-tery	Cost	ENF
F	lot12	lot9	lot11	lot3	lot5	6.5	2
G	lot12	lot7	lot11	lot3	lot5	5.8	9

The pareto set has just changed; F and G together are now pareto-superior to all prior solutions. Relaxing the slope constraint has paid off!

The relaxation of criteria can help us examine design alternatives that lie outside the original solution space. This exploratory process can uncover designs that turn out to be better than the original ones. When a designer, through a design process, finds a suitable solution, he might decide to stop or continue to explore. He might decide to explore in order to convince himself that the solutions he has are really the best, he does not want to miss the opportunity of finding something more interesting. A way of performing such an exploration is by relaxing the criteria on the problem. If criteria relaxation can be automated, then the computer can be used as an alternative generator. While, the computer

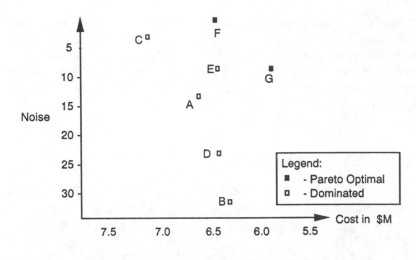

Figure 2-7: Pareto graph after marginal relaxation
of the slope criterion

can generate alternatives that may not be obvious to the designer, all alternatives, as far as the computer is concerned, are equally obvious.

How does one make the computer relax constraints? Traditionally, constraints have been expressed as predicates that either evaluate to true or false. For example, the constraint: *The homes should face south* can either be satisfied or not. If we are interested in relaxing the above constraint, we need some way of dealing with situations where the constraint is "almost" satisfied. It is not necessary that the homes face exactly south; slight deviations from south are acceptable. In order to allow such relaxations, the constraints can be converted into objectives. For example, the above constraint may be replaced with the following objective: *Minimize the deviation of the homes from the Southerly direction.* With this conversion, it now becomes possible to talk about a constraint as being partially satisfied.

We suggest that all the constraints be converted into an objective form. The set of all the original objectives and converted constraints are called *criteria*. The algorithms we will examine later (Chapter 5) evaluate design alternatives using all the given constraints and objectives. Tradeoffs are not made among objectives only, but among the constraints and objectives taken together. This approach allows users to make tradeoffs between relaxing constraints and increasing or decreasing the yield on objectives. Thus constraints and objectives are handled in an uniform fashion. Constraint relaxation and objective maximization/minimization are just two sides of the same coin.

Finding a new problem

After determining the cost of designs F and G to be $6.5M and $5.8M, respectively, our problem solver has now uncovered a new problem: Designs F and G place the single family homes on lot11 after relaxing the slope constraint. This means that extra cost is going to be incurred in making homes on steeper ground. Assume that the extra cost is going to $0.9 million. After adding $0.9M to F and G, a new graph is plotted (figure 2-8). The new pareto set consists of F, C, E and B; making E, B and C pareto optimal once again. By recognizing the existence of a new problem, the problem solver has to reconsider choices that were dominated earlier.

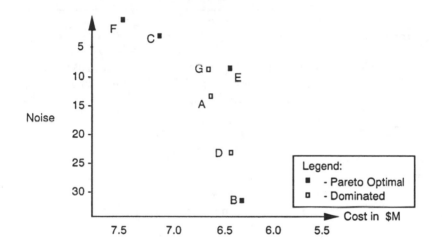

Figure 2-8: Building homes on steeper slopes is going to cost more

New Criteria

But wait! our problem solver has just changed his view about the now, pareto inferior design, G. In design G, the single family home complex is placed on a high slope that overlooks a wooded valley with a lake. This design resembles a similar design the problem solver has seen before. In the prior design, good view had been exploited to increase the value of the property. Drawing from this past experience, the problem solver new decides to introduce a new criterion to the current design problem:

8. The view from the homes should be good.

This new criterion is introduced as an additional dimension to the pareto space. The introduction of a new criteria in this fashion is called *criteria emergence* [Tomlin 86]. This is an important characteristic of innovative design. In the CYCLOPS system, new criteria emerge when the problem solver is reminded of a past case similar to the current design. The past case can be used to detect a problem or an opportunity in a design. The program uses a library of past experiences to find opportunities in the designs it generates. These past experiences are called *precedents* or *cases*[9].

Precedents are represented as frames containing the **conditions** of the experience, the **effects** of the conditions, and an **explanation** of how the conditions caused the effects.

Precedent#14

conditions: (home on high slope) AND (home over-looking valley)
AND (valley is wooded) AND (valley has lakes)
AND (home in Seattle)

effect: (very beautiful view)

explanation:

(very beautiful view) BECAUSE
(valley is beautiful) AND (home over-looking valley)

(valley is beautiful) BECAUSE
(valley is wooded) AND (valley has lakes)

Consider a precedent (precedent#14) about a house that has a nice view because it is high on a mountain slope overlooking a scenic valley. The **conditions** are a set of clauses that were true when the precedent was

---

[9]The words Precedent [Winston 81] and Case [Schank 77, Kolodner 80] will be used interchangeably.

acquired. A clause is a statement such as: *(home on high slope)*[10]. The **effect** is a set of clauses which denote the direct effects of the observed conditions. The **explanation** shows how the effect is associated to the initial conditions. It is expressed as a set of relations among clauses. In the example above, the first relation says that the view is beautiful because the valley is beautiful and because the home is overlooking the valley. The second one explains why the valley is considered beautiful. The purpose of the explanation will be addressed later in this chapter.

The above precedent can be used to identify a new criterion. For example, if the program encounters a situation that matches some of the **conditions** of the above precedent, the complete precedent is retrieved from memory. If the **explanation** of the precedent is found to verify against the current situation, then the corresponding **effect**: *(very beautiful view)* is inferred for the new situation and is used as a new criterion for evaluating the other design alternatives. In addition to discovering opportunities, precedents can also recognize problems. For example, if the system finds that some design alternative matches an unfavorable precedent, then a corresponding criterion is emerged.

In our example, we have two types of criteria: (1) criteria identified prior to designing *(prior-criteria)* and (2) *emergent-criteria*[11]. These two types of criteria are drawn from precedents. A question that one may ask in this context is: *If all criteria come from precedents, then why is it not possible to come up with all the criteria prior to designing? It's all in the designer's head anyway!* The problem is that, whenever a designer faces a new problem, everything in his Long Term Memory is potentially relevant. The designer cannot possibly take everything into account. He has to limit the scope of the problem by sticking to the domain of the current design. New criteria are retrieved from outside the domain only when some patterns in the current design causes the designer to be reminded of past cases in Long Term Memory. I faced the same problem while designing the CYCLOPS system. It is computationally intractable to search a design space using all past cases in Long Term Memory as design operators. The use of the precedent database has to be controlled by either limiting its use to certain parts of the design, or by having the conditions of newly

---

[10]This is not the exact representation used in the program; I have used a pseudo-English format for easy reading.

[11]A third class is criteria identified in the post-design phase. These criteria are realized by observing the performance of the designed artifact in the real world.

generated designs trigger the retrieval of past cases. In other words, if a certain design situation is similar to a past case, only then should the case be retrieved and used.

DESIGN ADAPTATION

Returning to the continuing example, lets assume our problem solver decides to work with design G, as it provides a good view. The design has a fault, however. It involves placing the homes on a steep slope, requiring some special action to be taken. In this section we will see how our problem solver might approach the problem by reasoning from past experiences.

Assume that the problem solver first tried to solve the problem by terracing the hillside. It then realized that terracing might lead to excessive erosion. Following, is a hypothetical "thinking aloud" protocol of how the problem solver might approach the problem:

Let's analyze the problem....

The homes at site11 are unfavorable BECAUSE they are on ground which is steeply sloped.

One approach is to get rid of the steepness by terracing the slope. This however, gives rise to erosion problems. What can be done next?

Let's see, the unfavorability is dependent on two reasons: *the homes are on the ground AND the ground is steeply sloped.* Negating the second reason with terracing did not work, what about negating the first reason?

Are there any cases in the database about not putting buildings on the ground.

.. long pause ..

Yes! There is a case about how people in Thailand keep their homes from getting wet during floods. They have devised a way of keeping their homes off the flood prone ground: they put their homes on stilts.

OK. Stilts should be used for the housing complex too. That seems like a good way of keeping a building off the ground.

Are there any new problems created? Do the new conditions cause the retrieval of any new cases? Are any criteria violated? If not, the design is acceptable.

Two precedents have been used here. First, the problem solver recognized that placing the house directly on the slope would cause the house to be unfavorably tilted. This could be recognized by a precedent that contains knowledge about how putting an object on a sloped surface makes the object tilted. After inferring the clause *(house is tilted)*, the problem solver starts looking for ways to solve the problem. It first searches a database of design rules. If no relevant rules are found, the case database is searched for cases that can address the "tilt" problem. In this scenario, let's assume that no relevant cases are found.

An approach to solving the problem under these conditions is to find the causes of the original problem. The idea is that, *if you cannot address a problem directly, try addressing its causes.* In our example, the causes of *(house is tilted)* are *(house on ground)* and *(ground is steep)*. The problem may now be solved by finding precedents that can help achieve either *(not (house on ground))* or *(not (ground is steep))*. Let us assume that the only precedent for the *(not(ground is steep))* is terracing, and that the terracing option has already been rejected. Alternatively, the requirement that *(not(house on ground))* triggers precedent #10, which is about how villagers in Thailand use stilts to protect their homes from flooding.

The precedent#10 is about the use of stilts to avoid flooding. But flooding is not our problem here, our problem is *(house on ground)*. However, if you examine the explanation of the precedent, you will find that one of the subgoals of precedents is to achieve *(not(house on ground))*. The associated action of the subgoal is *(action: house on stilts)*, which can be used to solve the steepness problem. Note that the purpose of using stilts in the precedent is very different from the purpose in the application. The program's ability to draw such analogies helps it solve design problems by drawing knowledge from a diverse set of precedents.

The final design, hence, is alternative G with the houses on stilts. The rest of the book provides theoretical and implementation details about the various issues touched upon in this scenario.

---

precedent #10

condition1: (ground is flooded) AND (house on ground)
            (house in Thailand)

effect1: (house is water-logged) AND (house is unfavorable)

action: (action: house on stilts) AND (action: stilts on ground)

effect2: (not (house is water-logged))

explanation:

(not (house is water-logged)) BECAUSE
(not (house on ground)) AND   (ground is flooded)

(not (house on ground)) BECAUSE
(action: house on stilts) AND (house on ground)

ASSUMPTIONS OF THE APPROACH

The approach and the implementation presented are based on the
following assumptions:

1. The design can be represented as a labeling problem.
   That is, the designed artifact consists of variables that
   have values assigned to them. Even though the number
   of variables can change during the design process, the
   assumption limits us to configuration-type designs.

2. The program does not actively verify analogies, it does
   not   perform   a   quantitative   or   qualitative
   simulation/analysis of the actions it takes. We felt this
   aspect was not central to our investigation. The program
   verifies analogies in a passive fashion. When an analogy
   is drawn, the modified design is posted to the precedents
   data-base. If none of the precedents find a problem, the
   analogy is deemed correct.   We make the further

assumption that any clause that cannot be inferred from the knowledge possessed is untrue. This is a *closed-world assumption* on the knowledge base. In other words: If you don't have the knowledge to recognize a problem, you **will** make the mistake of not recognizing the problem. No amount of sophistication in the reasoning mechanism can help. In the future, some standard simulation or analysis technique could be used for verification.

3. Currently, all criteria are treated equally. This problem is alleviated, to some extent, by using a dimensionless measure of utility. Finding appropriate weights for the various criteria is very difficult. If even one weight is incorrect, the system might miss good design solutions. In CYCLOPS, the effect of choosing wrong weights has been reduced (not eliminated) by the program's ability to relax criteria. In effect, if a particular criterion has a slightly lower weight than it ought to, then relaxations on other criteria will give the criterion its due consideration.

4. The precedent's explanations are hand-coded. The explanation assigned to a precedent predetermines how the precedent may be used.

5. Learning is limited to storing and re-using designs that are successfully executed by the program. CYCLOPS does not generalize.

6. CYCLOPS has only a limited knowledge base. Innovations the program makes are with respect to the knowledge the program has and not with respect to current state of the art in the domain of inquiry.

SUMMARY

This chapter presented some of the major ideas of the book with the aid of a hypothetical landscape design scenario. It followed the steps taken by a hypothetical problem solver as it went about solving a design problem, introducing these key issues:

• Certain design problems, such as landscape planning, can be represented as **configuration problems**.

- **Search** can be used as a means of solving discrete design problems.

- Design problems that have **multiple criteria** often require **tradeoffs** among criteria, which can be identified using a **pareto optimality** based evaluator.

- Optimal designs can be found by using **optimistic estimates** for the values of the objectives. This idea is a multi-objective variation of the standard A^* search algorithm.

- **Exploration** is an important part of design and that exploration in a space is the product of systematic **constraint relaxation**.

- **New criteria** can emerge during the design process. Such criteria can come from the past experiences of the problem solver.

- **Past experiences** can be represented as data structures called precedents. Typically, a precedent is represented as having: (1) a description of the conditions, (2) the effects of the conditions, and (3) an explanation of how the conditions cause the effects.

- Precedents can be used to solve design problems both directly and **analogically**. This is based on a technique that tries to address the causes of a problem if the problem cannot be solved directly.

- Criteria-relaxation based exploration, coupled with **knowledge based adaptation** can lead to **innovative** designs.

Chapter 3
The Design Problem

Formulating a design task as a computer solvable problem involves two major steps: choosing a representation for the artifact, and choosing a representation for the criteria that will be used to evaluate generated solutions. The formulation we use is based on the classic labeling problem [Waltz 75]. The labeling idea has been extended to suit the design domain by adding the notions of consistency [Nadel 85a] and optimization [Navinchandra 86a].

DESIGN REPRESENTATION

In order to design and to talk about design, it is important to be able to represent and communicate the design. The most common representation is a two dimensional sketch. An architect's sketch of a building, an engineer's drawing of a turret lathe, and a musician's composition of a symphony are examples of two dimensional (2D) representations.

A 2D representation, at the basic level, is composed of lines and points. At a slightly higher level, a 2D representation can be viewed as a collection of graphical primitives such as rectangles, circles, arcs, and curves. At an even higher level, the 2D representation could be a set of relationships among objects such as tables, chairs, fasteners, walls, doors, and columns. This hierarchy of representations points towards a particular class of design problems known as *configuration* design. An artifact is said to be configured if it is made by combining objects that are chosen from a given finite set of generic components. The final configuration satisfies a given set of criteria, expressed either as constraints or objectives. For example, a job-shop schedule can be viewed as a configuration of jobs that satisfies a given set of time and resource constraints. In another example, preparing a financial portfolio can also be viewed as a configuration task, in which, one assigns monies to different investments such that a given set of constraints and objectives are satisfied.

Not all designs are configurations. For example, the design of a baroque Venetian vase is composed of a complex collection of convex and concave surfaces. These surfaces, though mathematically definable, are not drawn from some finite set of primitives. Such a design cannot be said to be configured, rather, it is said to be formed. I call this kind of design *formative*.

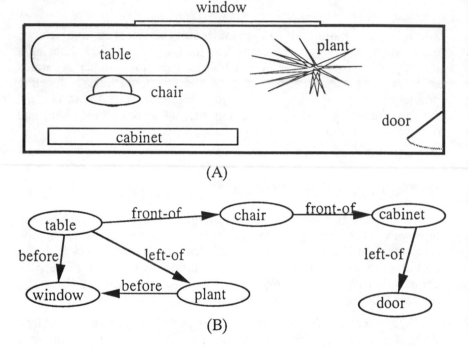

Figure 3-1: Layout language example

All the examples in this book concentrate only on simple two-dimensional artifacts. These can be represented by a class of representational formalisms known as *layout languages*. A layout language is essentially a set of propositions about a design. The propositions represent relationships among objects that make up the artifact. There are several applications of layout languages: equipment layout in a computer facility [Pfefferkorn 75], building layout [Habraken 83, Gross 86], and component layout on a VLSI chip [Soukup 81]. An example of a layout and its representation is provided in Figure 3-1. Part (A) of the Figure 3-1 is a plan view of a room. Part (B) of the figure shows a set of relations. Each object (depicted as an oval) contains a description of its own dimensions, its orientation and its location. The relationships depict inter-object distance, relative orientation, and direction. The layout language used in the example is ad-hoc; as there is no universal layout language. Researchers usually design layout languages to suit their own particular problems. The purpose for using a layout language is to provide a framework with which designs can be generated and tested for legality. We will be representing our landscape designs as sets of assignments of landuses to plots of land. Implicit in this representation is the notion of a layout language, as we will be using predicates to test inter-object relations such as distance, visibility, and bearing.

DESIGN AS A LABELING PROBLEM

In Chapter 2, we worked through a landscape design problem that was formulated as a configuration task. In the example, the designer had to assign each of the given set of landuses to one of a set of suitable sites. This representation is uni-dimensional. The design process involves assigning lots to landuses. When we say: "the apartment-complex is located at lot9", there is no notion of where lot9 is, or what direction the apartment complex faces. Inter-relationships among landuses are not a part of the representation. In fact, the full design can be expressed as a two-column table with the first column being the landuse's name and the second column being the name of the lot to which the corresponding landuse is assigned. This special type of configuration problem is called a *labeling problem* [Waltz 75, Nadel 85a]. The landuses are like variables and the lots are like values that can be assigned to the variables. The act of assigning a value to a variable is known as "labeling" the variable.

Labeling problems are amenable to automation. If a computer is given a labeling problem, all it need do is to randomly pick labels (values) for all the variables. Achieving a legal labeling, however, requires the computer to have some way of evaluating the alternatives it generates. One way of doing this is to provide the computer with a set of constraints with which it can screen labeling. When a labeling satisfies all the constraints it is said to be consistent. When constraints are added to a labeling problem, it is called a consistent labeling problem [Waltz 75, Nadel 85a].

The Consistent Labeling Problem has received much attention in Artificial Intelligence and Operations Research. The CLP was first introduced in two seminal papers [Walker 60, Golomb and Baumert 65]. Over the years, the CLP formalism has been successfully applied to a wide variety of problems.   One of the important applications of consistent labeling has been machine vision, and scene analysis in particular. Given an image of a scene that is comprised of several regularly shaped blocks, the computer is supposed to find out how many blocks are in the scene, even if the blocks partially obscure one another. Scene analysis involves three major steps: line/edge detection, line labeling and object interpretation. All three steps have been formulated as CLPs [Waltz 75, Haralick 80, Barrow & Tenenbaum 76] respectively. The CLP formalism is also well suited for dealing with graphs.   Applications include the map-coloring problem [Nijenhius and Wilf 75], the bin packing problem [Deutsch 66], and crypt arithmetic [Burstall 69]. For a complete list of applications and for a formal treatment of the CLP, refer to the work of Nadel [Nadel 85a, Nadel 85b, Nadel 85c, Nadel 85d].

In the Artificial Intelligence literature the Consistent Labeling Problem (CLP) is formulated as shown below[12]: (Adapted from [Nadel 85a])

1. There is a set of variables.

2. Each variable has an associated set of possible legal values. These sets are known as the **domains** (or **ranges**) of the variables.

3. There is a set of constraints on the values that various combinations of variables may compatibly take on.

4. The goal is to find one, or all ways in which values may be assigned to the variables such that the constraints are satisfied.

A landscape design problem can be represented as the following CLP:

1. There is a set of landuses that are to be sited.

2. Each landuse is to be assigned to a lot of land which is chosen from a set of given possible assignments.

3. There is a set of constraints on the lots assigned to the landuses.

---

[12]A formal, mathematical formulation of the CLP is provided in Appendix A

4. The problem is to find few (or all) ways of assigning landuses to lots such that the constraints are all simultaneously satisfied.

REPRESENTING A CLP IN THE COMPUTER

Consider the following example:

---

1. There are three variables: x_1, x_2 and x_3

2. Their corresponding domains are: $d_{x_1} = \{0, 1\}$, $d_{x_2} = \{1, 2, 3\}$ and $d_{x_3} = \{a, b\}$.

3. The constraints on a labeling are:

    a. $(2x_1)^2 + x_2^2 \quad >= \quad 5$

    b. $e^{-(x_1 + x_2)} \quad <= \quad 0.05$

    c. x_2 and x_3 should be chosen according to the following compatibility matrix: ("1" stands for compatible, and "0" for incompatible.)

	x2 = 1	x2 = 2	x2 = 3
x3 = a	0	1	0
x3 = b	1	0	1

d. $\cosh(x_2) > 2$

The constraints on a CLP need not be linear, polynomial or monotonic. Further, constraints need not be numeric at all. In the CLP above, the third constraint (c), is symbolic and cannot be expressed as <u>one</u> equation. Characteristics such as these make the CLP different from its close cousin, Integer Programming. Algorithms developed for Integer Programming problems assume continuous convex constraints. For many problems, particularly design, this can be a serious limitation. The CLP technique, on the other hand, makes fewer assumptions about the problems it solves and is more general than standard discrete value methods. The CLP, however, is not without problems. There is no elegant analytic technique for solving CLPs. Techniques in use today are based on search which is, by nature, a weak method. We are forced to use weak methods because the CLP formulation makes so few assumptions about the constraints it handles. This is in contrast to certain Integer Programming algorithms which assume linear constraints and are able to exploit that linearity in order to find solutions. Search techniques for solving CLPs are discussed in the next chapter.

In the example above, we have a mixture of numeric and symbolic variables. Constraints among numeric variables are easily expressed as equations. For symbolic variables, however, a different form of predicate is required. We have found compatibility matrices to be a fairly general way of representing relationships among variables[13] Even some complex design criteria that are non-numeric or non-monotonic are easily expressed as matrices. For example, if one is scheduling manpower in a job-shop situation, one might want to make sure that the workers assigned to the same time slots are compatible and get along (socially) with one another. A matrix could be used to easily represent this constraint. Constraints such as these, on the other hand, could also be formulated as equations, but not without unnecessary complexity.

We will express all design criteria as compatibility matrices. This allows us to develop a general solution technique that can be used for problems, regardless of the type of variables or criteria. The constraints introduced in the example above can be converted into matrices as shown below.

(a) Equation $(2x_1)^2 + x_2^2 \geq 5$ is converted into the following table which relates the compatibility between the domains of x_1 and x_2. This table is called a *compatibility matrix*.

	x2 = 1	x2 = 2	x2 = 3
x1 = 0	0	0	1
x1 = 1	1	1	1

---

[13]Much work has been done on understanding CLPs with constraints that relate only two variables [Mackworth 77]. Such constraints are called binary. Binary constraints are used because they are easy to represent and use. CLP solution techniques developed for binary constraints are usually applicable to *n*-ary constraints. An *n*-ary constraint is represented as a *n*-dimensional compatibility matrix.

(b) $e^{-(2x_1 + x_2)}$ <=   0.05

	x2 = 1	x2 = 2	x2 = 3
x1 = 0	0	0	1
x1 = 1	1	1	1

(c) This constraint is already in the form of a compatibility matrix:

	x2 = 1	x2 = 2	x2 = 3
x1 = 0	0	1	0
x1 = 1	1	0	1

(d) $\cosh(x_2) > 2.0$

x2 = 1	x2 = 2	x2 = 3
0	1	1

In the example above, there are only three consistent labelings for x_1, x_2 and x_3: (1 2 a), (0 3 b), and (1 3 b), respectively.

OPTIMIZATION AND THE CLP

When we design an artifact, we would like the product to not only satisfy all the constraints, but also to be a good design. A particular design can be said to be better than other designs only if there is some method for comparing designs. The CLP formalism introduced in the previous section has no notion of "best" solution. Its goal is to find a labeling that satisfies all the constraints. Real world design problems, however, are not mere constraint satisfaction problems, they often involve multiple objectives. Here are some examples of objectives in different design domains:

- **Financial Portfolio design**: minimize risk, maximize diversification

- **Landscape design**: minimize cost, maximize access, minimize noise

- **Machine design**: minimize cost, minimize weight, minimize vibration

- **Diet design**: minimize fat, maximize nutrition, maximize variety

- **Structural Member Design**: minimize weight, minimize cost

Many instances of the above design problems could be formulated as CLPs with the addition of an optimization component. I call the new formulation a Consistent Labeling Optimization Problem (CLOP):

1. There is a set of variables.

2. Each variable has associated with it, a finite set of values known as its domain.

3. There is a set of constraints on the variables, that evaluate to either true or false.

4. There is a set of objectives that evaluate to a finite number.

5. The goal is to find a few (or all) ways to assign to each variable, a value from its associated domain in such a way that all the constraints are simultaneously satisfied and all the objectives are simultaneously either maximized or minimized.

Representing objectives

In the section on constraint representation (Page 43) it was shown how constraints can be represented as compatibility matrices. We will now see how objectives can also be represented as compatibility matrices, in keeping with our desire to represent constraints and objectives in a similar fashion.

Refer back to the CLP presented on page 43. The problem had three variables and four constraints. The addition of the following two objectives converts the CLP into a CLOP:

- **Objective 1.** The first objective is symbolic and, let's assume, is based on some subjective reason.

  Given that x_2 can take one of the values {1 2 3} and x_3 can take one of {a b}, a list of compatibilities among the variables is shown below. The measures of compatibility are: highly compatible, just compatible, moderately compatible and incompatible. The preferences on the values of x_2 and x_3 are:

  - a is highly compatible with values 1 and 2

  - a is just compatible with value 3

  - b is highly compatible with 3 but moderately compatible with 1

  - b is incompatible with 2

  The objective is to maximize the compatibility between the labelings chosen for x_2 and x_3.

- **Objective 2.** Maximize the function: $\log(x_1 + x_2)$

This CLOP example can be solved by first listing down all the solutions to the corresponding CLP and then selecting the optimal. The CLP has three consistent labelings for x_1, x_2, and x_3 : (1 2 a), (0 3 b) and (1 3 b). Let's determine which one is optimal.

Just as we converted complex constraints into compatibility matrices, the objectives can also be be represented in this fashion. Let's start with the first objective.

Conversion of the first objective: There are four types of relationships among the values in the x_2 and x_3 domains: highly-compatible, just-compatible, moderately-compatible, and incompatible. These four relations are assigned ranks 1, 2, 3, and 4. The lower the rank the better. The matrix is as follows:

	x2 = 1	x2 = 2	x2 = 3
x3 = a	1	1	2
x3 = b	3	4	1

The combinations of x_2 and x_3 that maximize the objective are (1 a), (2 a), and (3 b).

Conversion of the second objective: The second objective is an equation that can be evaluated and expressed as a table:

	x2 = 1	x2 = 2	x2 = 3
x1 = 0	0.0	0.3	0.47
x1 = 1	0.3	0.47	0.6

The value 0.6 is the maximum and should be assigned a rank of 1. All other boxes, being sub-optimal, are ranked with with numbers greater than 1 . The best rank is achieved by the labelings $x_1 = 1$ and $x_2 = 3$. Consequently, the solution (1 3 b) emerges as the only consistent labeling that maximizes both the objectives (achieves a rank of 1) simultaneously, making it a solution to the given CLOP.

In the chapters to come, design will be treated as a CLOP, with the constraints and objectives represented as matrices.

SUMMARY

Formulating a design problem involves two major steps: choosing a representation for the design, and choosing a representation for the criteria that will be used to evaluate the designs.

Representation. Certain design problems can be viewed as configuration tasks. An artifact is said to be configured if it is made by combining objects selected from a given finite set of generic components. The designer's task is to find a configuration that satisfies a given set of criteria. A landscape design problem is a configuration task that can be formulated as a labeling problem. A labeling task involves assigning values to a given set of variables that represent the design. The value assigned to a particular variable has to be selected from a pre-defined set associated with that variable.

Evaluation. The evaluation of designs is based on a set of criteria consisting of constraints and objectives. A labeling problem with constraints is called a consistent labeling problem (CLP), and a CLP with objectives is called a consistent labeling optimization problem (CLOP).

As design problems can involve symbolic and numeric variables, and as the governing constraints and objectives can be non-linear, non-monotonic and even non-continuous, we need an elegant way of representing the constraints and objectives. We have found compatibility matrices to be a fairly general way of representing relationships among variables. Even some complex design criteria that are non-numeric or non-monotonic are easily expressed as matrices. For example, if one is scheduling manpower in a job-shop situation, one might want to make sure that the workers assigned to the same time slots are compatible and get along (socially) with one another. A matrix could be used to easily represent this constraint.

All design criteria are expressed as compatibility matrices. This allows the development of a general solution technique that can be used for problems regardless of the type of criteria involved.

CONCLUSIONS

In the CLOP example described above, we found only one consistent labeling that maximized both the objectives simultaneously. The criteria used in the example were carefully selected to yield this final solution. This, however, is not possible in real world problems. In practice, there can be many objectives all preferring different solutions. Under these circumstances, choosing any one solution requires that different objectives be traded off against one another. This raises several questions: How are tradeoffs identified? What techniques can we use to find optimal solutions when there are multiple criteria? Can such techniques yield global optimal solutions or should we settle for local optima? The next chapter addresses these questions, among others; and presents a search-based solution technique for consistent labeling optimization problems.

Chapter 4
Design Synthesis

Synthesis is the process of composing and combining parts to form a whole. It is the process by which design solutions are generated. From a methodological point of view, synthesis can be viewed as a heuristic search process.

Search techniques have been successfully applied to a variety of configuration design problems. Though very general in its applicability, search is a slow and inefficient method of finding solutions. Much of the research in this field is directed towards finding clever methods of reducing the size of the search space. This chapter presents one such method for solving design tasks which are formulated as Consistent Labeling Optimization Problems (CLOP).

This chapter introduces the notion of synthesis by searching. It introduces examples about *labeling* with constraints and objectives. We will examine a new algorithm called *Pareto Optimal-A**, which is a modified form of the standard A^* algorithm and can be used for to find optimal solutions to problems with multiple objectives.

SEARCH AS ENUMERATION

Search techniques can be used to enumerate points in the space of all possible combinations. In our implementation, solutions are generated by performing a tree-like search. For example, if we had three variables x1, x2, and x3 with domains {1 2}, {a b c}, and {x y}, respectively. Labelings in the state space can be generated as shown in Figure 4-1. The leaves of the tree represent labelings. There are twelve labelings in all. Had there been some constraints on the solutions, then the consistent labelings would have been from among these twelve solutions.

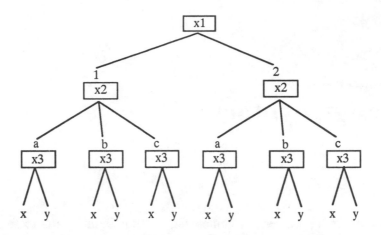

Figure 4-1: The state space

A way of generating consistent labelings is to use the *generate and test* paradigm [Lindsay 80]. The generator continuously produces labelings and the tester checks them for consistency. When the first consistent labeling is found, the process stops.

A better approach, for design problems, is to search for solutions in a tree like fashion; checking for consistency during the synthesis process rather than at the end. Examples of techniques that use this approach are depth-first search [Golomb 65], breadth first search and constraint directed search [Fox 83]. To illustrate the use of search in design synthesis, we will work through a simplified version of our landscape design example. Treat this new example independent of the one presented in the Scenario (Chapter 2).

THE EXAMPLE PROBLEM STATEMENT

Three facilities are to be sited: a dumpsite, an apartment-complex, and a single-family housing complex. The set of possible labelings for the three landuses are shown below, and the corresponding map is shown in Figure 4-2.

variable	domain (list of lot numbers)
apts	(5 7 9 10 11 12 17)
housing	(5 9 10 11 12 17)
dump	(3 5 7 9 10 11 12 17)

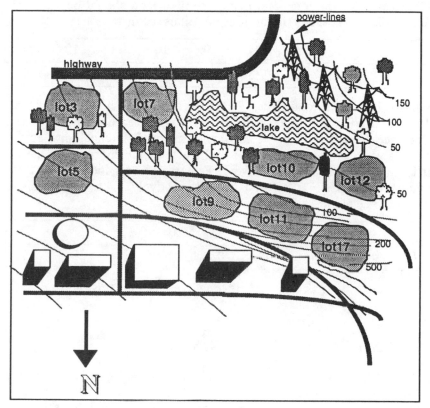

Figure 4-2: Example map

There are four constraints:

Constraint 1: The slope of the lot should be less than or equal to 8% for all three landuses. The actual % slopes for the lots are shown below:

lots:	3	5	7	9	10	11	12	17
slope:	2%	3%	2%	4%	6%	10%	7%	14%

Constraint 2: The soil conditions should be good. The soil conditions of the different lots is shown in the table below (Key: 1 = good, 2 = moderate, 3 = poor):

lots:	3	5	7	9	10	11	12	17
soil:	1	1	1	1	2	1	3	1

Constraint 3: The total cost of all acquired land should be less than $35 Million. The costs (in millions of dollars) of the lots are:

lots:	3	5	7	9	10	11	12	17
cost($M):	13	13	8	10	17	10	14	8

Constraint 4: The total Excess Noise Factor (ENF) should be less than 15. The ENF is the total of the excess noise at each of the facilities. The excess noise for a particular facility is the difference between the acceptable noise for the facility and the actual ambient noise of the lot it is sited at. The acceptable Noise Factors (NF) for the apts, housing and dump are 22NF, 18NF and 28NF respectively. The noise levels at each of the sites are:

lots:	3	5	7	9	10	11	12	17
NF:	45	30	30	20	22	20	22	20

The goal is to find a consistent labeling over all four constraints.

SEARCHING FOR A SOLUTION

Let us start solving the above problem using a *depth-first* strategy [Golomb 65]. The search is carried out successively, selecting variables and then selecting members from the variable's associated domain. Each member is treated as an alternate value for the variable. Each alternative forms a branch of the tree. The first variable is **apts** and the expanded tree is shown in Figure 4-3.

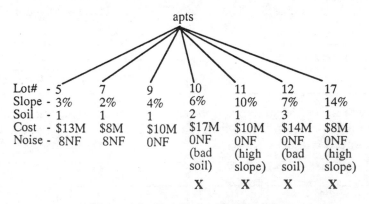

Figure 4-3: Variable "apts" expanded

At the end of each branch there are five numbers: the lot number, the percent slope, the rank of the soil type, the total cost, and finally the ENF[14] . After laying out these numbers, a constraints check is performed. In the figure, X's appear under the branches that violate any one of the four constraints. In other words, they represent inconsistent labelings and are *pruned* off the search tree.

The process of branching and pruning is continued till a complete solution is found. The final solution (apts = 5, housing = 9 and dump = 7) is shown in Figure 4-4. This consistent labeling is found by searching in a depth first fashion, expanding the left-most branch at every stage. In the first stage, there are seven alternate locations for the apartments. Only three of these alternatives are consistent with the constraints. In the second stage, the left-most consistent alternative is expanded. There are six alternate locations for the housing complex. The left-most alternative, Lot 5, is rejected because the apartments have already been placed there. The next location, Lot 9, is checked for consistency and expanded. This process continues till a complete, and consistent solution is found.

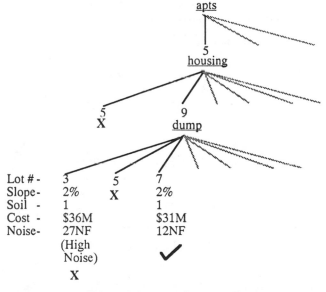

Figure 4-4: A consistent labeling

---

[14]Computed as the difference of the actual noise at the site and the acceptable noise level of the corresponding landuse.

This example shows how designs can be synthesized using a simple search technique. There are other more sophisticated methods[15] for handling constraints and constraint satisfaction problems. In the research presented here, it has been our aim to study design exploration and innovation and consequently we have used a simple search technique which adequately serves our purposes. In the context of our research goals it was felt that pursuing sophisticated, efficiency improving techniques was not going to qualitatively change our results.

LOOKING FOR OPTIMAL CONSISTENT LABELINGS

We will now convert the CLP presented on page 52 into an optimization problem. The revised problem statement is shown below. The revision involves converting the cost and noise constraints into objectives. The other two constraints are left unchanged.

As before, there are three facilities to be sited a dumpsite, an apartment-complex, and a single-family housing complex. The set of possible labelings for the three landuses are shown below:

variable	domain (list of lot numbers)
apts	(5 7 9 10 11 12 17)
housing	(5 9 10 11 12 17)
dump	(3 5 7 9 10 11 12 17)

The first two constraints are unchanged:

Constraint 1: The slope of the lot should be less than or equal to 8% for all three landuses. The actual % slopes are shown below:

lots:	3	5	7	9	10	11	12	17
slope:	2%	3%	2%	4%	6%	10%	7%	14%

Constraint 2: The soil condition should be good.

---

[15]Such methods include: dependency-directed backtracking [Stallman & Sussman 77], constraint-directed search [Fox 83], constraint-posting [Stefik 80, Navinchandra 86b], generalized backtracking [Golomb 65], forward-checking [Nadel 85d].

lots:	3	5	7	9	10	11	12	17
soil:	1	1	1	1	2	1	3	1

Key: 1 = good, 2 = moderate, 3 = poor

The cost and noise constraints are now converted into objectives:

Objective 1: The total cost should be minimized. The costs (in millions of dollars) of the lots are:

lots:	3	5	7	9	10	11	12	17
cost($M):	13	13	8	10	17	10	14	8

Objective 2: The ENF should be minimized. The acceptable Noise Factors (NF) for the apts, housing and dump are 22 NF, 18 NF, and 28 NF respectively. The noise levels at each of the sites are:

lots:	3	5	7	9	10	11	12	17
NF:	45	30	30	20	22	20	22	20

The goal is to find a consistent labeling that simultaneously minimizes both objectives.

A good search algorithm for finding optimal solutions is the A^* algorithm [Hart, Nilsson & Raphael 68]. The A^* algorithm is defined for problems with a single objective function. The CLOP, however, is a multi-objective optimization problem which involves finding the non-dominated set of complete designs. In this section we will see how the A^* algorithm can be extended to find optimal solutions using pareto-optimality[16] as a measure of goodness. This extended algorithm is called *Pareto Optimal-A^* (PO-A^*)*.

The standard A^* is a best-first algorithm where the "goodness" of a node, $f^*(n)$, is the sum of the actual cost of reaching that node $g(n)$, and the optimistic estimated cost of reaching the solution from that node, $h^*(n)$. The first complete solution A^* finds is guaranteed to be optimal provided, $\overline{h^*}(n)$ is always an optimistic estimate. Algorithms used to find $h^*(n)$ that satisfy this condition are said to be A^* - *admissible*.

---

[16]We shall use the phrases pareto optimal and non-dominated interchangeably.

The *PO-A*[*] algorithm uses pareto optimality to determine the "goodness" of a node. All pareto optimal nodes are expanded at each stage of the search (unless the user chooses otherwise). The <u>first</u> complete solution found is guaranteed to be pareto optimal over the entire space of solutions. The admissibility of *PO-A*[*] is based on using optimistic estimates of the values for each of the criteria in the CLOP. This means that *a particular node will be PO-A*[*] *admissible over the entire search tree if the values of the criteria that govern it are individually A*[*] *admissible.* This condition is necessary and sufficient for obtaining solutions which are pareto optimal over the entire search space. A proof of this result is provided in Appendix A.

The *Pareto Optimal-A*[*] algorithm is a slightly modified form of the the standard *A*[*] algorithm [Nillson 71]. A comparison of the two algorithms is shown in Figure 4-5.

We will now work through an example to illustrate the *PO-A*[*] algorithm. The process starts by expanding the domain of any one of the variables. Once again, let us start with the **apartments**. The resulting tree is shown in Figure 4-6[17]. The technique used for calculating the ENF and the cost (shown in the figure) is based on an admissible heuristic.

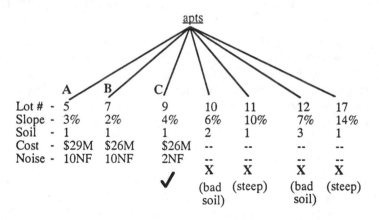

Figure 4-6: Expanding "apts"

In the previous section we calculated the cost of a node as the total cost incurred till that node. We used this cost to prune the tree and search

---

[17]The reader is urged not to stop to verify all the numbers. Just try to get an intuitive understanding of the algorithm, the arithmetic is not important.

The A* algorithm:

1 Put the start node 's' on a list, called OPEN, of unexpanded nodes. Calculate f^* and associate its value with node s.

2 If OPEN is empty, exit with failure; no solution exists.

3 Select from OPEN a node 'i' at which f^* is minimum. If several nodes qualify, choose a goal node if there is one, and otherwise choose among them arbitrarily.

4 Remove node 'i' from OPEN and place it on a list, called CLOSED, of expanded nodes.

5 IF 'i' is a complete solution, exit with success; a globally optimal solution has been found.

6 Expand node 'i', creating nodes for all its successors. For each successor node 'j' of 'i'

  a. Calculate f^* (j)

  b. Add 'j' to OPEN and attach a pointer from 'j' back to its predecessor. (in order to trace back a solution path once a goal node is found).

7 Go to (2)

The PO-A* algorithm:

1 Put the start node 's' on a list, called OPEN, of unexpanded nodes. Calculate $f^*(s)_1, f^*(s)_2 \ldots \ldots f^*(s)_n$. (Where, $f^*(p)_q$ is an optimistic heuristic estimate of the final value that would be attained by the qth criterion given the pth node.)

2 If OPEN is empty, exit with failure; no solution exists.

3 Select from OPEN a node 'i' which is <u>non-dominated</u>. If several nodes qualify, choose a goal node if there is one, and otherwise choose among them arbitrarily.

4 Remove node 'i' from OPEN and place it on a list, called CLOSED, of expanded nodes.

5 IF 'i' is a complete solution, exit with success; a globally optimal solution has been found.

6 Expand node 'i', creating nodes for all its successors. For each successor node 'j' of 'i'

  a. Calculate $f^*(j)_1, f^*(j)_2 \ldots \ldots f^*(j)_n$

  b. Add 'j' to OPEN and attach a pointer from 'j' back to its predecessor. (in order to trace back a solution path once a goal node is found).

7 Go to (2)

Figure 4-5: Comparison of A^* and *PO-A**

forward. As this cost is only partial, it often happens that the search goes down paths that eventually lead to dead ends. This problem could be eliminated if one could accurately determine the actual cost of completing a given partial design. This determination, however, is not possible – at least, not without actually completing the design. We can, however, try to estimate the cost to completion.

Let the estimated total cost of a particular branch/node (n) be composed of two parts: $g(n)$ and $h^*(n)$, where, $g(n)$ is the total cost incurred till the node, and $h^*(n)$ is an optimistic estimate of how much more might be incurred in achieving the goal. The total estimated cost $f^*(n)$ is given by:

$$f^*(n) = g(n) + h^*(n)$$

We will adopt a heuristic approach for estimating $h^*(n)$. For a given partial design, there are usually a number of variables which have yet to be determined. Let's call these the *future variables* [Nadel 85b]. As we don't know, ahead of time, what values these variables will take, it is not possible to determine how much it will cost to complete the partial design. The heuristic we use assumes that each future variable will be assigned a value from its domain that is the best value with respect to the objective function (e.g., cost). For example, let's calculate the $f^*(n)$ of node "B" in Figure 4-6 (page 58). The cost of choosing lot 7 is $8M (a given). This is the $g(n)$ of the branch. At this stage there are two more landuses yet to be sited: housing and dumpsite. Their domains are now {5 9 10 11 12 17} and {3 5 9 10 11 12 17} and the corresponding costs are {13M 10M 17M 10M 14M 8M} and {13M 13M 10M 17M 10M 14M 8M}, respectively.

In order to calculate $h^*(n)$, we make the assumption that the housing and the dumpsite will be located at the cheapest of the available sites[18], and that no additional costs will be incurred in doing so. In our example, $h^*(n)$ is calculated by assuming that the housing is placed on the cheapest site - lot 17, and the dump is placed on the remaining cheapest site - lot 11.

This makes $h^*(n) = (8 + 10) = $18M, and

$$f^*(n) = g(n) + h^*(n) = 8 + 18 = $26M$$

---

[18]One might ask: "Where did you get the heuristic from?" The answer is simple: Heuristics often do not have sound, provable origins. There is no analytic way of telling whether a given heuristic is either good or bad. A heuristic is good as long as it is in use and no other heuristic refutes it by showing better search efficiencies.

The same is done for the calculation of total Excess Noise Factor (ENF). As CLOPs have finite domains for their variables, it is always possible to use the above heuristic to calculate $h^*(n)$.

Having examined how criteria values are estimated, we can now return to the example. We last expanded variable, **apts** (Figure 4-6) we have to now choose the best branch and expand it further. Branch 9 (C) has the lowest NF but branch 7 (B) has the lowest cost. Which one do we choose? A tradeoff has to be made between noise and cost. This can be done using a Pareto Graph. The three partial labelings are plotted on a graph as shown in Figure 4-7. Solution C is *pareto optimal*, it dominates solutions A and B.

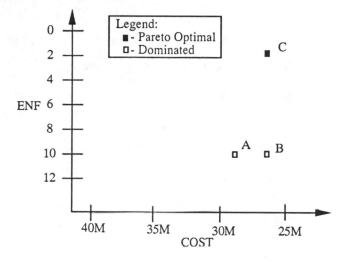

Figure 4-7: Plot of the first three consistent partial solutions.

Solution C is expanded first. Figure 4-8 shows alternate locations for the housing complex. Only one partial solution (D) satisfies the constraints. The new pareto optimal design is now B.

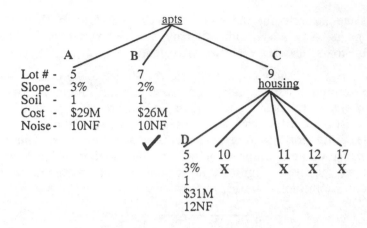

Figure 4-8: Expanding "housing"

The search now has to backtrack to solution B and expand that node. This is shown in Figure 4-9. Two new consistent solutions, E and F, have been generated.

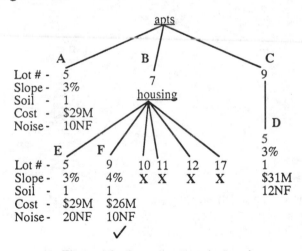

Figure 4-9: Expanding "housing" again

To enter the next stage of the search, all the unexpanded nodes (A, E, F and D) are plotted on a pareto graph and the dominating solutions are identified. In this case, solution F has lower cost and lower noise than all the other solutions. As F is the dominant solution, it is expanded next. This is shown in Figure 4-10. Two new consistent solutions have been generated, G and H. These solutions are complete. Once again, a pareto optimality check is applied to all unexpanded nodes and the two complete solutions.

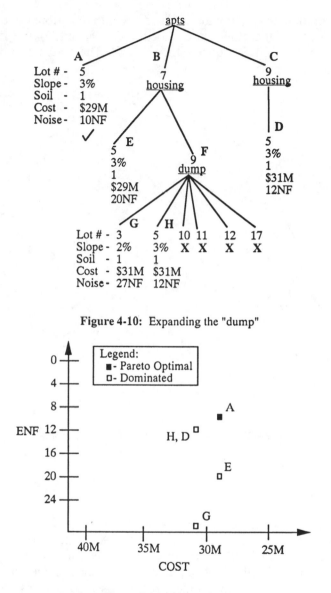

Figure 4-10: Expanding the "dump"

Figure 4-11: Pareto Graph

The solutions in question are plotted on a Pareto Graph as shown in Figure 4-11. Solution A is pareto optimal, and is chosen for expansion. Two stages later, the search tree has four complete solutions, as shown in Figure 4-12. This time, the Pareto Optimal solutions are K, E, H, and D. The solutions K and H are the only complete pareto optimal ones. According to the *PO-A** algorithm, the first complete pareto optimal solution to be found is guaranteed to be globally optimal. Expanding any of the other unexpanded nodes (E and D) will not lead to a solution that will dominate either K or H. The reader may wish to verify this.

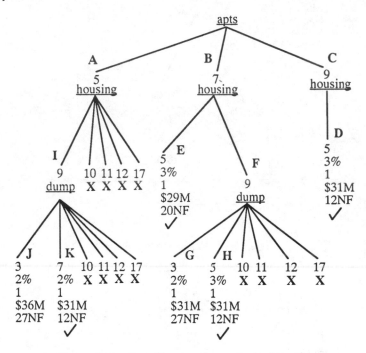

Figure 4-12: Two Complete Pareto Optimal Designs

SUMMARY

Search proceeds in stages. Each variable expansion is a stage in the process of synthesizing complete solutions. A design which has been cast as a CLP or a CLOP is said to be complete when all its variables have been instantiated. The path leading to each node in the tree (except for the bottom-most nodes) represents a partial design. Each stage of the search process adds more detail (new instantiations) to the partial designs. This is the process of synthesis, as shown in Figure 4-13. Partial designs are fed into a synthesis module, where details are added. Detailed designs which are incomplete, re-enter the loop and go through the process till completion.

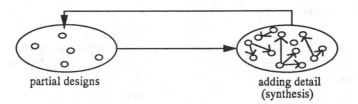

Figure 4-13: The Labeling Process

The process shown in Figure 4-13 is capable of generating all labelings. If a consistency check is added, it becomes a CLP solver (Figure 4-14).

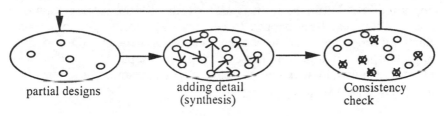

Figure 4-14: The Consistent Labeling Process

After a consistency check, if we use pareto optimality with optimistic estimates, we get a CLOP solver, as shown in Figure 4-15. Note that the consistency check prunes the bad partial designs (indicated by X's) but the pareto optimality check only suppresses pareto inferior solutions (indicated by little boxes). Pareto inferior solutions are not pruned off because they have a chance of becoming pareto optimal as the synthesis proceeds. As designs accumulate detail, the pareto surface either stays unchanged or might slowly migrate towards the origin. The Pareto Surface cannot move away from the origin because it is based on optimistically estimated values. Adding detail to the partial designs is not going to improve their ratings over the optimistic estimates[19].

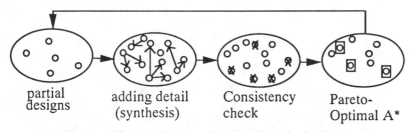

Figure 4-15: The Consistent Labeling Optimization Process

---

[19]A formal proof of this phenomenon is provided in Appendix A.

CONCLUSION

In this chapter we seen have how A^* search and pareto optimality are used together to generate solutions to Consistent Labeling Optimization Problems. The technique is called PO-A^* (Pareto-Optimal A^*). A formal treatment of this algorithm is provided in Appendix A.

The PO-A^* algorithm is based on dividing the search space into two sets: the dominated and the non-dominated. The algorithm treats all pareto-optimal solutions alike, even if some of them are at the extremes. This behavior serves design exploration well, for extreme solutions can sometimes serendipitously lead to new criteria and hidden opportunities. Furthermore, it is also worthwhile to explore solutions that are dominated but happen to be very close to the pareto surface. Such solutions can lead to the emergence of new criteria and new opportunities different from those available in the pareto set. For these reasons, we would like our program to also examine solutions just below the pareto surface.

Chapter 5
Design Exploration

Exploration is the process of generating and evaluating design alternatives that normally would not be considered. Normal synthesis processes, such as search, are aimed at considering only those design alternatives that are within the solution space defined by the governing criteria. An exploratory process, on the other hand, tries to generate a wide variety of alternatives from outside the solution space, some of which may unearth new opportunities or solve design problems in unexpected ways.

Exploration is not guaranteed to unearth better designs; the best designs may lie within the solution space. One cannot, however, be sure of that unless one actually explores beyond it; which is why exploration is an important part of innovation. If you limit yourself to the solution space defined by the design criteria, you limit yourself to producing designs within the design culture of the domain. We called this kind of design puzzle solving. To be innovative, one has to try to step outside one's design culture and break one's mindset about "appropriate" types of technologies and techniques. Remember, the key to innovation is being different.

The process of innovative design isn't the mere satisfaction of given criteria. The selection and refinement of criteria is very much part of the design process. Take the case of an architect who is given the problem of redesigning a neighborhood to reduce crime. As the specifications are incomplete, the architect has to elaborate the specifications and develop a strategy for approaching the design. Even in better specified problems, instead of blindly adhering to the given specifications, designers often like to explore the possibilities and examine their options. The aim is to arrive at an overall good solution to the given task, even if it means changing the specifications. For example, consider another architect who is given the task of locating townhouses on a site. Assume that the site is located near the edge of a cliff, and overlooks a valley. The owner's specifications require that there be a fixed number of units, each with a view of the valley and all within the budget. These specifications are incomplete. The architect, drawing from his past experiences, might decide to consider additional criteria about noise, access, privacy and safety. Taking these specifications, the designer might decide to place all the houses along the cliff's edge, in order to give each unit a good view of the valley. While working on this layout, the designer might recognize the opportunity for a mini golf-course in the middle of the site. Seeing this, he might decide to change the specifications and add some more houses to the originally specified number and have them face the golf course instead of the valley. In this way, the designer may arrive at, what he believes to be a good solution; even if it requires altering the specifications. "The shape of the design space appears to be determined as much by the search process itself as by external factors .... The definition of design spaces is therefore dynamic, and the design process involves not only search within such spaces but the acquisition and modification of the knowledge that defines those spaces." Quoted from: [Coyne et.al. 89].

In this chapter we will examine a computer based technique for exploration. The proposed technique explores outside the solution space by relaxing the criteria that bound the space. Alternatives generated by criteria relaxation are examined for opportunities. This is done by comparing the new design alternatives to past experiences. If an opportunity is found, then a corresponding new criterion is added to the original design specification. The emergence of criteria during the design process can sometimes change the focus of the problem solving task and can lead to solutions completely different from what a normal synthesis technique would produce. Criteria relaxation and criteria emergence are the central ideas of our approach to design exploration.

A SCENARIO

You have just been admitted to an urban university as a graduate student. Your first assignment, and probably the toughest in college, is to find off-campus housing. You go to a realtor and place the following criteria before him:

- Constraint1: Monthly rental of the studio should be less than or equal to $400.

- Constraint2: The place should be no more than a 15 minute walk to school.

- Objective1: I want the largest studio.

- Objective2: I want the quietest studio you have.

The realtor has only four studios that satisfy both constraints. After some discussion, you decide to go look at them. The first studio, on River Street, is large but close to a noisy highway. The second, on Harvard Street, is a small studio tucked away in a large apartment complex located in a relatively quiet neighborhood. The third, on Main Street, is noisy and small. Finally, the fourth, on Brattle St, is relatively quiet and of medium size. You have a clear tradeoff among the apartments on River Street, Brattle Street, and Harvard Street, - a tradeoff between noise and size. The Main Street apartment is inferior to all the other choices. The plot in Figure 5-1 illustrates this situation graphically, with a curve drawn through the non-dominated points. This curve is called the *pareto curve*.

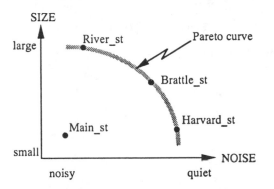

Figure 5-1: Trading-off noise and and size

Having seen the four houses, you are now confused and indecisive. The realtor then starts taking you to a fifth studio:

"Where are you taking me now?"

"I have a fifth place that I'd like to show you"

"Is it less than $400 a month?"

"Come with me and check this place out"

"How much does it cost? I need to know!"

"Why don't we look at the place first. If you don't like it you don't have to take it."

"Oh well, if you insist."

The fifth house, on Brookline street, is medium sized and relatively quiet, however, it is dominated by the Brattle street apartment. This is shown in Figure 5-2.

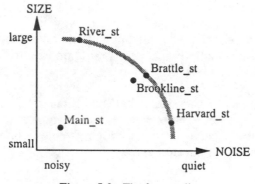

Figure 5-2: The four studios

The conversation continues:

"Do you like the place?"

"Yes! But how much?"

"Do you have a car?"

"No."

"This is a good place sir, it's a 10 minute walk to school from here and you are only 3 minutes from the Subway station. The other four places are very far from public transportation."

"Hmm... I don't have a car, I really do need to be close to public transportation."

"The Central Square bus station is only three minutes away, a large grocery store is also within four to five minutes of here. You like this place, sir?"

"Yes! This place is really convenient. I had not thought of these other things in my original list of criteria. So, how much?"

"Four twenty five"

Things have changed, there is a new objective to consider. You now want a studio with minimum distance to public transportation. This new objective can be represented as a third dimension in the Pareto Graph.

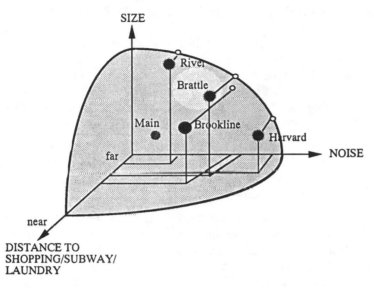

Figure 5-3: A new criterion

Let us assume that only Brookline Street fares well on the third objective. It goes from being a dominated alternative to being on the pareto surface. Which of the three studios would you now choose?

In this scenario, by relaxing the constraint on rent we are lead to consider the Brookline Street studio, which turns out to be favorable because it had very easy access to public transportation. A new objective is introduced.

The same happens in design. When constraints are relaxed, new design alternatives come into consideration. It is possible that some of these new designs evoke, in the designers mind, some new criteria that change the terms of evaluation and choice. The alternatives generated by constraint relaxation serve as cues that may give the designer a new idea. This is the *Emergent Criteria* phenomenon [Tomlin 86].

In the conversation above, notice how the realtor insists that you see the fifth studio. He hopes that it has certain characteristics that catch your fancy. Note how he avoids questions about its actual price. He is afraid that if he tells you the price up front, you will discard the alternative immediately. He hopes you will relax the cost criterion *after* looking at the studio. The program (CYCLOPS) adopts a similar approach.

EXPLORATION IN DESIGN: SOME INTUITIONS

In this book, criteria relaxation is proposed as a means of exploring design alternatives.   The proposed technique explores outside the normal solution space by relaxing the constraints and objectives that bound the space. In effect, relaxation increases the size of the solution space allowing us to examine designs in the state space which would normally have been pruned off.

There are two common types of criteria in design problems: constraints and objectives. Both these criteria define the solution space as a subset of the larger space of all possible designs. We can explore the space by relaxing either of these criteria:

Constraint Relaxation overcomes the artificial precision built into a criterion. For example, remember our landscape planner who relaxes the constraint that "all homes be on slopes less than 8%" to some higher value, say 10%. He makes available to him, plots of land that are on slopes between 8% and 10%. It is possible that some of these new alternatives may provide opportunities such as better soil conditions or better view. When we say that the slope should be less than 8%, it does not mean that lots with slightly higher slopes, say 9% or 10%, should be completely avoided.

Objective Relaxation. Objective functions are usually required to be either maximized or minimized. For this discussion let's assume all objectives are to be maximized. The maximum value of an objective can achieve, taken independently, is called its *ideal* value.   When binding constraints are presented, the maximum value is lower than or at best, equal to the ideal. This is called the *constrained optimal*. If there are other objectives, one may not be able to attain even the constrained optimal, and may have to settle for a *pareto optimal*. In constrained, multi-objective design problems, objectives may be relaxed in two ways: by *Tradeoff* and by *Slipping*. A tradeoff occurs when one pareto optimal alternative is chosen over another. A tradeoff implies relaxing (lowering) one's expectations on one objective to get a higher value on another.

The other way to relax objectives is to deliberately push the pareto surface down towards the origin, bringing design alternatives that were less than pareto optimal to the surface. I call this kind of relaxation, shown in Figure 5-4, *slipping*. In Part A only a few of a large group of designs are non-dominated and lie on the pareto surface. The pareto surface defines the tradeoff between objectives **O1** and **O2**. The objectives may be relaxed by deliberately pushing the pareto surface towards the origin. In effect, all solutions which lie just below the pareto surface become available for consideration. An important property of this technique is that it prefers to surface designs that are very close to being non-dominated.

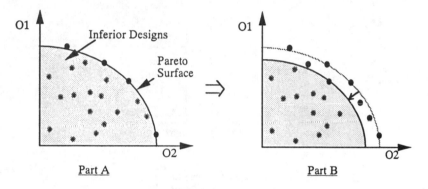

Figure 5-4: Pareto Slip

We now have a notion of how constraint relaxation and objective relaxation can be used to generate design alternatives. The question is, Are these two relaxation types related? If so, how?, And: What is their relation to design? How does one decide when to relax constraints and when to relax objectives?

Criteria: Representation and Relaxation

The notion of relaxation is not new. Researchers in Operations Research have developed methods for relaxing objectives. The literature on multi-objective problem solving abounds with techniques for managing and presenting tradeoffs among objectives [Goicoechea 82]. A question I like to ask is: "If we are amenable to relaxing objectives by trading off among them, then why are we so rigid about the constraints on the problem?"

When tradeoffs are being made, it essentially means that we are bargaining among different viewpoints. Why then, should constraints be treated as sacrosanct? Why shouldn't they be included in the bargaining and trading-off process? To address this problem, we have developed a simple, unified method for representing, using, and relaxing constraints and objectives alike. This is done by converting constraints and objectives into a generalized form called the *criterion*. Instead of being simply satisfied or not-satisfied, a criterion has several levels of satisfaction. The various levels are identified and ranked to indicate which levels are better than others.

Consider the objective to minimize the cost of design. This may be rewritten as: "Maximize the closeness of the actual cost to the theoretical minimum." Graphically, the reformulation is as shown in Figure 5-5.

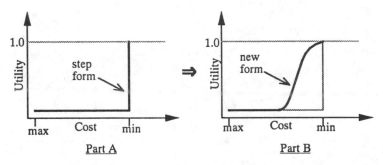

Figure 5-5: From a step change to a relaxed change

Part A shows how we normally specify objectives. An objective is said to be satisfied if and only if its value is at the extremum. In the figure, the utility of obtaining the minimum is unity and any other value, higher than the minimum, has zero utility. This form of representation in a multi-objective problem makes it difficult to find solutions that satisfy all the objectives simultaneously. However, it is possible to find solutions that are in the neighborhood of the theoretical optimal. Such solutions achieve values close to the extremum, with correspondingly lower utilities. This concept is illustrated in Part B of Figure 5-5. The figure shows how a sharp step change is converted into a smooth, relaxed one. In the current implementation the relaxed form of a criterion is represented as a matrix of ranks. This is done by assigning ranks to ranges of utility.

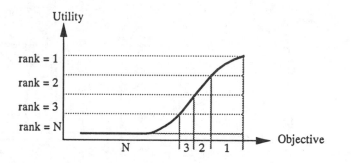

Figure 5-6: Ranks and ranges of utility

In the figure above, regions (ranges) are assigned ranks. A design whose objective value falls within a region is assigned the corresponding rank for the objective in question. The best value obtainable is assigned a rank of 1. The region just next to the best is assigned a rank of 2, the next best region is assigned a rank of 3 and so on. This is carried out till some lower bound is reached. Values lower than the lower bound are assigned rank N. Where, N indicates "Not-to-be-considered". In the program, N is set to a very large number which, in effect, eliminates the region. A modified form of Figure 5-6 is shown below. The figure shows how the objective can be set up to reject any value below a predefined cutoff; all such values are assigned a rank of N.

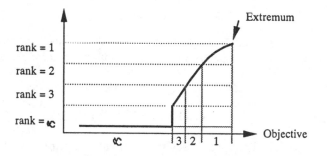

Figure 5-7: The function starts with a step and then smoothes out

The same idea can be extended to constraints. Consider the constraint: "Build homes only on south facing slopes." Rewording it as a criterion, we get: "Build homes facing a direction that has a bearing as close to the Southerly direction as possible." The transformation is shown below:

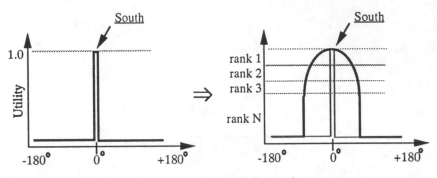

Figure 5-8: Homes facing south

In yet another example, the constraint: "Cost of housing <= $2M" can be changed into a ranked criterion as shown below:

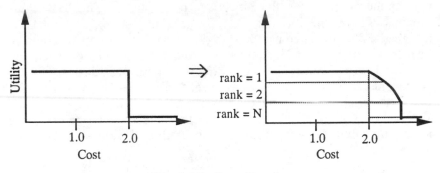

Figure 5-9: Cost of housing

Using this reformulation technique, we shall now return to the landscape example and re-solve the problem using criteria relaxation.

THE LANDSCAPE EXAMPLE, REVISITED

Let us redefine the Landscape design problem in light of what we have just discussed, converting the constraints and objectives into relaxable criteria.

As before, there are three facilities to be sited: a dumpsite, an apartment complex and a single-family housing complex. The sets of possible labelings for the three landuses are shown below:

variable	domain (list of lot numbers)
apts	(5 7 9 10 11 12 17)
housing	(5 9 10 11 12 17)
dump	(3 5 7 9 10 11 12 17)

Criterion 1: The slope of the lot should be less than or equal to 8% for all three landuses. The actual % slopes are shown below:

lots:	3	5	7	9	10	11	12	17
slope:	2%	3%	2%	4%	6%	10%	7%	14%

The above values are to be ranked. Any site with slope less than or equal to 8% is assigned a rank of 1. The sites 11 and 17 have to be assigned worse ranks. If we adopt a five-rank scale, then the best value of 8% is assigned a rank of 1 and the rank 5 is assigned to the worst: 14%. By linear interpolation, the 10% slope is assigned a rank of 2. The ranked matrix is shown below:

lots:	3	5	7	9	10	11	12	17
slope:	1	1	1	1	1	2	1	5

Criterion 2: The soil ranks for each of the landuses should be equal to 1.

lots:	3	5	7	9	10	11	12	17
soil:	1	1	1	1	2	1	3	1

Criterion 3: The total cost is to be minimized. The costs (in millions of dollars) of the lots are:

lots:	3	5	7	9	10	11	12	17
Cost($M):	13	13	8	10	17	10	14	8

These too can be ranked on a scale of 1 to 5:

lots:	3	5	7	9	10	11	12	17
cost:	3	3	1	2	5	2	4	1

Criterion 4: The ENF[20] should be minimized. The acceptable Noise Factors (NF) for the apts, housing and dump are 22NF, 18NF and 28NF respectively. The noise levels at each of the sites are:

lots:	3	5	7	9	10	11	12	17
NF:	45	30	30	20	22	20	22	20

The differences in the NF of the site and the landuses is tabulated below:

lots:	3	5	7	9	10	11	12	17
apts:		+8	+8	-2	0	-2	0	-2
housing:		+12		+2	+4	+2	+4	+2
dump:	+17	+2	+2	-8	-6	-8	-6	-8

The total ENF that is to be minimized is dependent upon positive deviation of the NF of a lot and the acceptable NF of the landuse sited there. The above table shows the differences in NF for all the possible sitings. The best rank of 1 is be assigned to a NF difference of zero or less. The NF differences +20 and above are assigned a rank of N. The worst NF difference of +17 is assigned a rank of 5 and all other ranks are obtained by linear interpolation. The resulting rank matrix is shown below:

lots:	3	5	7	9	10	11	12	17
apts:		3	3	1	1	1	1	1
housing:		4		1	2	1	2	1
dump:	5	1	1	1	1	1	1	1

The aim is to find a labeling such that the rank attained by each of the given criteria is equal to unity.

---

[20]As defined before, the ENF is the total of the excess noise at each of the facilities. The excess noise for a particular facility is the difference between the acceptable noise for the facility and the actual noise of the lot it is sited at.

Solution Process

We shall use $PO\text{-}A^*$ to solve the above problem. The search is carried out by choosing variables and expanding their domains into branches. The branches are then evaluated and the pareto optimal set is extracted for the next stage of the search. In order to ensure optimality, the branches are evaluated using optimistic estimates of the costs of completion.

The first variable is "apts" and the expanded tree is shown in the figure below:

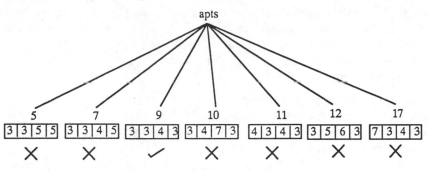

Figure 5-10: Expanding "apts"

At the end of each branch there is a box with four numbers, representing the rankings attained by the four criteria: slope, soil, cost and noise. This set of values is called the *spectrum* of the partial design. Consider the third branch: (9) for a moment, let's examine how the values in the corresponding spectra are calculated.

slope: The decision to place "apts" at lot "9" yields a slope rank = 1 (page 77). As we are using $PO\text{-}A^*$, we need to estimate (optimistically) the ranks for "housing" and "dump". We can make the assumption that the rest of the facilities will be sited at the best of the available lots: 3 and 5. The estimated slope rank is:

$$f^*(n)_{slope} = g(n)_{slope} + h^*(n)_{slope}$$
$$f^*(9)_{slope} = g(9)_{slope} + h^*(9)_{slope}$$
$$f^*(9)_{slope} = 1 + (1 + 1) = 3$$

The first box on branch "9" is a three.

soil: The soil rank is calculated in the same fashion

cost: The decision to place "apts" at lot "9" yields a cost rank =

2. The best lots available for the dump and housing are 17 and 7.

$$f^*(9)_{cost} = g(9)_{cost} + h^*(9)_{cost}$$

$$f^*(9)_{cost} = 2 + (1 + 1) = 4$$

noise: The noise rank is calculated in same way.

Having expanded all the branches, the next step is to select the best branch to expand further. This is done by finding the pareto optimal set. Pareto optimality is now based on four criteria: slope, soil, cost and noise. Comparing the spectra of the branches in Figure 5-10, we find that branch 9 dominates all other branches (Xs are marked under the dominated alternatives). The next step, according to the *PO-A*** algorithm, is to expand the non-dominated branches and to continue the process till complete solutions are found.

The expansion is shown in Figure 5-11. Unfortunately, all the newly generated partial solutions are dominated. The pareto optimal solutions are branches 7, 10, 11, and 12. The next step, according to the algorithm is to expand <u>all</u> the non-dominated branches. But this step causes problems. As the *PO-A*** algorithm expands the full non-dominated set at each stage of the search, it produces too many alternatives at each stage making it unsuitable for interactive situations. As we wish to have the designer examine alternatives and look for opportunities in them, we cannot overwhelm him. A way of alleviating this problem is to order the non-dominated set using some measure of "goodness" and to then expand the best, first. The idea is to avoid examining the complete non-dominated set all at once, but to examine the set in some order. The question is, what order? Are some pareto optimal solutions more optimal than others? What other measure can we use?

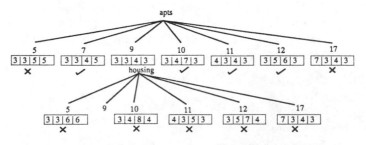

Figure 5-11: Expanding the Non-Dominated partial solution

Ordering the Non-dominated Set

We order the non-dominated set based on deviations from the ideal solution. Consider three partial solutions A, B, and C, which have the following spectra:

```
A (  2   5   3   4   6   3   2)
B (  1   4   2   1   5   1   2)
C ( 78   2  35  45  81  72  11)
```

In the set above, B dominates A. Solution C, which has very poor ranks in its spectrum has one criterion with such a good rank that it cannot be dominated. As a result, B and C are pareto optimal. Clearly, C is an extreme solution, as it has much worse ranks than B on all but one of the criteria. For this reason, it is desirable to expand B before C. It is important to note, however, that we do not want to eliminate C, we only want to postpone its examination, as it has only one good rank in its spectrum. We don't eliminate C altogether, because it could lead to an interesting solution. We do not want the algorithm to eliminate any opportunity, no matter how remote. The decision whether or not to eventually examine C should lie with the user.

The ordering technique we have used is based on a simple measure of deviation of a solution from the ideal. The best spectrum for a partial design is one with all ranks equal to one. Let's call this the zero[th] order optimal design. The second best spectrum is one that has one of its criteria attaining a rank of two. Let's call this a first order optimality. We can use the order of a design to select designs from sets of pareto-optimal designs. Let's see how this is done:

The spectrum of a design i is indicated by S_i:

$$S_i = \{ s_{i1}, s_{i2}, \ldots s_{in} \}$$

Where s_{ij} is the rank attained by the jth criterion in the spectrum S_i. If the total number of criteria is n, then the order of the spectrum (Δ) is given by:

$$\Delta = \sum_{j=1}^{n} w_j (s_{ij} - 1) \tag{5.1}$$

Where w_j is the weight attached to the jth criterion. In the current implementation all weights are set to unity.

Using Δ for search. We shall now modify the *PO-A*[*] algorithm using the measure Δ, for ordering the non-dominated set. The modified algorithm is called *Ordered Pareto Optimal-A*[*] *(OPO-A*[*]). The

OPO-A* algorithm uses a threshold value of Δ (denoted by Δ_g) as a means of limiting the search. The search process is similar to *PO-A**, the difference being that instead of expanding the complete non-dominated set, we now expand only those branches in the non-dominated set that have a Δ less than or equal to the threshold (Δ_g). Before the search starts, Δ_g is set to 0. The search starts by expanding the root node that has a Δ of 0 (most optimistic). The search process continues till the first complete non-dominated solution is found or till there are no branches with Δ less than or equal to Δ_g. If the process stops with no solutions, Δ_g is incremented and the search restarts from where it last stopped. The process is then continued till a complete non-dominated solution is found. The first such solution found is guaranteed to be pareto optimal (non-dominated) over the entire state space[21]. The algorithm is shown below:

OPO-A* Algorithm:

　1.　Put the start node s on a list, called *OPEN*, of unexpanded nodes. Calculate $r^*(s)_1, r^*(s)_2, \ldots, r^*(s)_n$ and associate its value with node s. (Where, $r^*(p)_q$ is an optimistic heuristic estimate of the final rank that would be attained by the qth criterion given the pth node.)

　2. Calculate the Δ value for each node p, where

$$\Delta = \sum_{i=1}^{n} (r^*(p)_i - 1)$$

　3. Set the threshold Δ_g to 0.

　4. If *OPEN* is empty, exit with failure; no solution exists.

　5a. Select from OPEN non-dominated nodes with $\Delta \leq \Delta_g$. Call this set *ND*. Remove the *ND* nodes from *OPEN* and place them in a list of expanded nodes called *CLOSED*.

　5b. If no non-dominated nodes with $\Delta \leq \Delta_g$ exist, increase Δ_g by one and go to Step 4. (One may halt the algorithm here to ask the user if Δ_g should be increased and by how much).

　6. If any node in *ND* is a complete solution (all variables

---

[21]A proof of this result is provided in Appendix A

instantiated), exit with success; a globally optimal solution has been found. If more solutions are needed, remove the optimal solution from *ND* and repeat this step. If *ND* has no complete solutions go to the next step.

7. Expand the nodes in *ND*, creating new nodes for the successors. For each successor node j of each node i in *ND*:

a. Calculate $r^*(j)_1, r^*(j)_2, \ldots, r^*(j)_n$ (the spectrum of j).

b. Add j to *OPEN* and attach a pointer from j back to its predecessor (this is to trace back a solution path once a goal node is found).

8. Go to Step 4.

Interestingly, the process of increasing the threshold, as described above, serves as a means of performing systematic criteria relaxation! As we accept designs with higher Δ we are, in effect, moving away from the theoretical best and gradually lowering our expectation on the values attainable in the designs' spectra. Considering designs with higher values in their spectra means that the governing criteria are being relaxed. Hence, the process of gradually increasing Δ_g, to bring higher order solutions into consideration, is equivalent to criteria relaxation. This process of increasing the threshold is how CYCLOPS explores new alternatives. In the rest of this section we will work through an example to illustrate the *OPO-A** algorithm.

Returning to the Layout Example

The last branching is shown again in Figure 5-12 with the Δ values calculated for the nodes. Of the four non-dominated solutions, the lowest Δ is 10. This means that Δ_g will have to be increased to 10 before any new branching can begin.

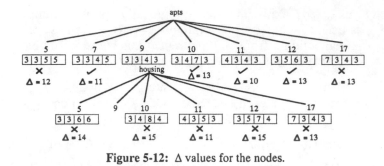

Figure 5-12: Δ values for the nodes.

Setting Δ_g to 10, the next branching is shown in Figure 5-13

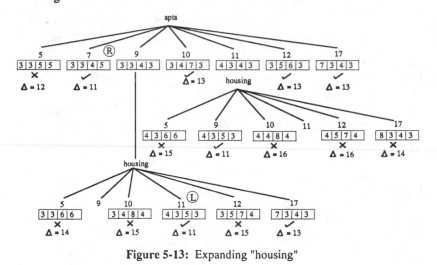

Figure 5-13: Expanding "housing"

The non-dominated set now has seven members. The algorithm comes to a stop as there are no non-dominated nodes with a Δ less than or equal to the current Δ_g of 10. The Δ_g has to be relaxed to a higher value, say 11. The nodes **R** and **L** qualify. Picking the more complete node (**L**), the next expansion is shown in Figure 5-14.

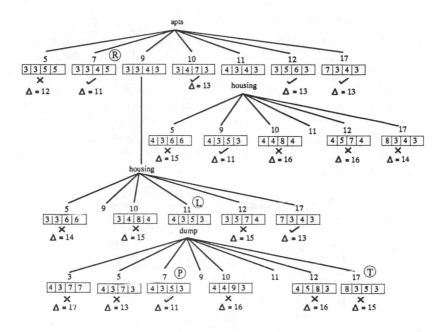

Figure 5-14: Expanding "dump"

Of the eight non-dominated designs there is one goal node (**P**) with a Δ equal to the current Δ_g. As it is a complete and non-dominated solution, it is guaranteed to be Pareto Optimal over the entire search space. An optimal solution, hence is: apartments at Lot9, Housing at Lot11, and the Dump on Lot7. The total cost of this design is \$28M and the total noise level is only 4 NF.

Let's see how these designs compare to designs found earlier. In the previous chapter the final design was: apts on lot7, housing on lot9, and dump on lot5, (page 63) with a cost of \$31M and a total ENF of 12. In that chapter, all the designs which used the relatively steeper lot 11 were eliminated by the slope constraint. In the current example, by relaxing the slope constraint, we have a design that is both cheaper and less noisy. Note that the relaxation was not performed directly on the constraint. We just raised the Δ_g threshold to consider alternatives that, in turn, contained relaxations. Raising the threshold automatically relaxes constraints and objectives. This gives us a convenient and easy-to-use exploration method.

The relaxation process need not stop as soon as an optimal is found. It is always possible that further relaxation may yield something interesting.

Relax, and hope for the best

A relaxation can be applied at any stage of the solution process. Let's relax the problem by increasing Δ_g arbitrarily to 13. Several new non-dominated designs can be considered. This expansion of node **R** (Δ = 11) and node **S** (Δ = 13) is shown in Figure 5-15. Node **S** is chosen over other nodes of the same Δ value because it is closer to completion. The expansion produces another optimal solution **Q**. This solution is even cheaper than the solution **P** found in Figure 5-14. Solution **Q**, however, does very poorly with respect to the slope constraint. The ultimate tradeoff lies with the user.

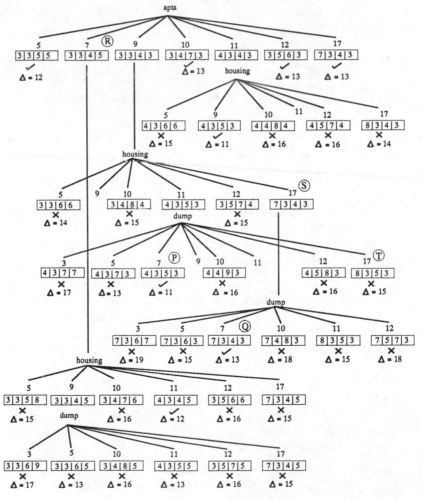

Figure 5-15: A Relaxation

This demonstrates how constraint relaxation can unearth potentially good designs even after some solutions have been found[22]. Furthermore, criteria relaxation can generate alternatives which turn out to be interesting in some unexpected way. This is possible even though the new alternative compromises the specified criteria. A new alternative may have certain characteristics that cause the observer to be reminded of some favorable past experience, making the observed design favorable. The sudden recognition of a design as being favorable (or unfavorable) is equivalent to adding a new criterion to the design problem. This phenomenon is termed *criteria emergence*.

CRITERIA EMERGENCE

Criteria can emerge during the design process. For example, while considering a given design alternative, a landscape designer might recognize that the design provides an excellent view. Assuming he had not considered view as a criterion earlier, he might decide to make "good view" one of his considerations for selecting a design. Such re-specifications can often change the focus of the designing process.

Let us now return to the continuing example and see how new criteria could emerge during design. In the last synthesis step (Figure 5-15), we had two non-dominated solutions, **P** and **Q**:

	apts	hsng.	dump	Δ	$	NF	slope	soil
P	9	11	7	11	28	4	high	OK
Q	9	17	7	13	26	4	very high	OK

A tradeoff has to be made between slope and cost. Are these the only criteria for selection? Let's check if any new criteria can be emerged. Referring back to the map (Page 53), we can see that placing the housing complex on Lot 17 will give the homes a very good view of the valley. We never had view as one of our criteria, so let's introduce a new criterion to the spectrum of each design. All high altitude lots facing the valley will score good ranks on this new criterion. Lot 17 is the highest and will score the best.

---

[22]This phenomenon is repeated several times in the trace of the program CYCLOPS (refer Appendix B).

Using this new criterion, all the other designs are re-evaluated. This will cause some previously dominated solutions to become pareto optimal. For example, solution **T** in Figure 5-15, which has a cost of $28M and a noise level of only 2NF! It is now up to the user to decide how he wants to tradeoff view, noise, cost and slope. Had a relaxation not been made, the system would not have surfaced this alternative and the new criterion "good-view" would not have emerged, and a good opportunity would have been lost. This is true regardless of whether this particular alternative is ultimately selected or rejected.

Criteria emergence plays an important role in exploration. It helps in the recognition of interesting designs among the alternatives generated. Further, the new criteria which emerge during design need not always be favorable, they can also correspond to problems in a design. The recognition of problems plays an equally important role in exploration as it helps prune the space.

Where do new criteria come from? A good source happens to be the user. The system can rely on the user to recognize opportunities and potential dangers. The user may do this by drawing knowledge from his past experiences. For example, in the landscape design problem, the "good view" criterion could have been added as a result of the user being reminded of some similar past experience. He could have been reminded of a visit to a house that was located high on a hillside and overlooked a valley.

In this context, the user and the computer work together: The computer system generates alternatives and the user either rejects or accepts them, as he recognizes problems or opportunities. This approach, however, has a serious limitation: it puts a lot of burden on the user. An earlier implementation of CYCLOPS that had only the *OPO-A*[*] algorithm (with an interface) was difficult to use because it produced dozens of alternatives which the user had to scrutinize in detail to find the interesting ones. The process is tiring and time consuming for people. My experience with this early version of CYCLOPS led to the idea that if the computer had the relevant knowledge, it could help the designer by trying to recognize problems or opportunities by itself and then report them to the user. An advantage of this approach would be that the computer can be left to examine large numbers of alternatives leaving the designer free to work on other problems. It should be noted, however, that the program would be only in a position to suggest alternatives and all final decisions would be still left to the designer.

CYCLOPS' ability to recognize interesting designs and emerge new criteria based on a database of past experiences (precedents). The program matches given designs to the database. If a design has certain characteristics that match a precedent, then the precedent is retrieved and applied.

Precedents and Emergent Criteria

A precedent, in its simplest form, is a record of an experience or episode. More specifically, a precedent is a record of the conditions and the effects experienced. The effects may be either physical or emotional. All precedents are input by the programmer or knowledge engineer.

A precedent is represented as a frame [Minsky 75]. The frame based representation captures the conditions and effects experienced. The conditions describe the physical characteristics of the past experience, and the effects are the consequences of the conditions. The effects may be either physical or emotional. During evaluation, the system matches precedents to the current design. If a design is found to be similar to some past experience, then the corresponding effect is applied to the current design. The effects serve as criteria for evaluating new designs. If a new design matches a prior design with an unfavorable effect, then the new design is also assigned the same unfavorable effect. In this way, designs are evaluated in relation to prior experiences. The evaluations can include non-quantifiable effects such as good-view, commanding-position and awkward-looking. Justifications for such evaluation, lie not in some well founded domain theory, but on the mere existence of a similar prior experience. In spirit, it is like saying: "I know this arrangement of houses will look nice because I have seen something similar before, and it looked good then." We don't really try to represent the concept of aesthetics, we just keep a pointer to a similar prior case as justification.

In the scenario above, we saw how a designer might take a liking for a particular design because it reminds him of some favorable past experience. We would like the system to draw similar inferences from a computer database of past experiences. The "good view" criterion is emerged from a precedent which is represented in the system as follows:

Precedent#23

conditions: (home altitude high) AND (home view valley)
                 AND (valley has lakes) AND (valley has woods)

effect: (favorable: home good-view) AND (good-view rank -1)

The application of the precedent is quite simple. If the condition of the precedent matches[23] the condition of any design, then a new criterion is added. This new criterion is called "good-view" and is given a rank of -1 wherever it is satisfied. All other designs are assigned a rank of 1 (denoting no opportunity) by default[24]. In CYCLOPS, favorable conditions are given negative ranks and unfavorable conditions are positive. Neutral conditions are given a rank of unity. The ranks, in criteria such as soil and slope represent degrees of unfavorability. For example, in the slope constraint, a rank of 1 means there is *no problem* with the design. Ranks of 2 or 3, on the other hand, denote problems. Worse ranks represent increasing unfavorability. The "good-view" criterion, on the other hand, represents something favorable. The ranks used should not be measures of problems but should be measures of *opportunity*. As, an opportunity is the opposite of a problem, we use a ranking scheme opposite of that used for criteria representing problems. Consequently, in the "good-view" criterion, a rank of 1 will represent no opportunity, while, ranks of 0, -1, -2 and lower will represent increasing levels of favorability.

---

[23]This should not be confused with production rule based approaches. The CYCLOPS program bases inferences on recognizing similarities and drawing analogies among designs. This is because designs rarely have the exact same conditions. In those rare instances when a new design problem exactly matches a prior case, the precedent <u>is</u> used as a simple If-Then rule.

[24]Note that adding new criteria with rank = 1, does not change the Δ of a design.

Matching

The most important aspect of precedent based evaluation is matching. Matching is done at three levels: directly, through an abstraction and by looking up a thesaurus. The simplest match is a **direct** one, in which attributes of the base and target are the same.

The second type of matching used in CYCLOPS is the **abstract match**, where, the attributes of base and target are matched by moving up and/or down a predefined object and concept hierarchy (see Figure 5-16, Page 92). The only purpose of this hierarchy is to match clauses indirectly. CYCLOPS will match any two objects (at the leaves) that are separated by up to six links[25]. For example, a base about hotels might match a target about offices because they are both commercial buildings.

Finally, the system has a **thesaurus** to help match words of similar meanings. The thesaurus is represented as sets of words of similar meaning. For example, the word "sloped" will match "steep" as they both appear in the same set.

A more advanced form of matching used for case adaptation is described in the next chapter.

SUMMARY

Exploration is the basis of innovation. The process involves generating a wide variety of alternatives and then throwing away the uninteresting ones.

Design exploration can be done in several ways. The technique we have used is based on criteria relaxation. By relaxing the criteria that define the solution space, we can explore beyond that space. The technique is a modified form of the $PO\text{-}A^*$ algorithm. The first step in our algorithm is to convert all the constraints and objectives into relaxed criteria. The ways in which a given criterion can be relaxed is pre-determined. For example, the constraint: "Build homes only on South facing slopes" is converted into the following relaxed form: "Build homes facing a direction that has a bearing as close to South as possible". Objectives are also converted in this manner. For example, the objective: "Minimize the cost of the design" is manually converted

---

[25]There is no theoretical justification for the amount of relaxation allowed.

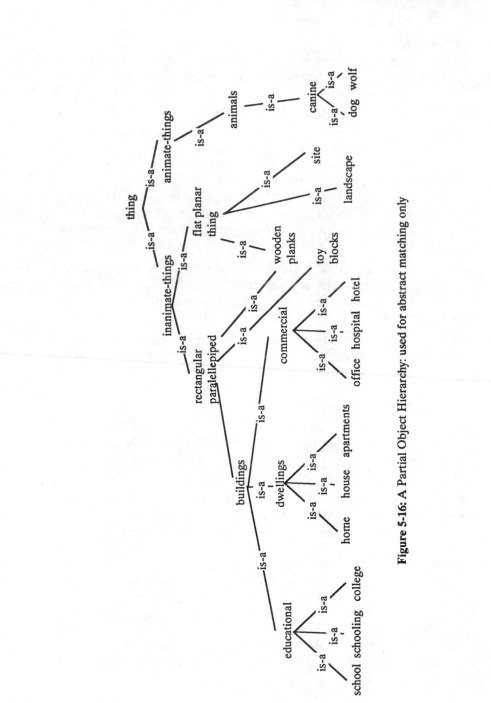

Figure 5-16: A Partial Object Hierarchy: used for abstract matching only

into the following form: "Maximize the closeness of the actual cost to the theoretical minimum". These conversions allow us to consider solutions that are in the neighborhood of the optimal, and that partially satisfy the constraints.

The next step is to use relaxation to explore sub-optimal design alternatives that are not normally considered. Some of these alternatives could, possibly, have hidden opportunities or characteristics that solve the design problem in an unexpected way.

In one mode of operation, the CYCLOPS program can be viewed as a generator of alternatives for the user who, based on his knowledge and experience, analyses each design for hidden problems or opportunities. However, as the number of alternatives can be very large, we must find a way of ordering our examination of alternatives, looking at the most promising ones first. We do this using the Ordered Pareto-Optimality algorithm, starting from zero[th] order optimality and slowly increasing the order so as to find solutions. It sometimes may be possible to find a final solution with all the criteria maximized simultaneously. In practice, however, we may be required to gradually increase Δ_g in order to find a basic first solution. The gradual increasing of Δ_g represents a gradual relaxing of one's expectations, where Δ_g becomes a cumulative measure of deviation from the ideal.

We also proposed focusing on the most promising alternatives by providing the program with the experiential knowledge it needs to recognize interesting designs. That database of experiences is made up of precedents. A precedent, in its simplest form, is represented as a frame which records the conditions of the experience and the effects of the conditions. While examining design alternatives, if CYCLOPS finds that a design's characteristics match a precedent, then the precedent is retrieved and applied. The effect of applying a precedent can either be favorable or unfavorable. For example, CYCLOPS might recognize that some design configuration provides a very good view, one that is not available in the other designs. When this happens, the program introduces a new criterion "view" into the design problem. This phenomenon of adding criteria during design, as a result of designing, is called criteria emergence. If CYCLOPS finds any such new opportunity, it reports the finding to the user.

It is through the combination of criteria relaxation and emergence that CYCLOPS performs design exploration.

Chapter 6
Design Adaptation

In the previous chapter we discussed how precedent-based knowledge can be used by a program while examining an alternative. This form of reasoning can be used not only for recognizing problems and opportunities, but also for adapting designs that have promise but need a few corrections. Precedents can be used to solve design problems either directly or analogically, as part of a process called design adaptation.

In the introductory chapter we argued that an innovative design system should have, at the least, the following three abilities:

- the ability to consider a wide variety of design alternatives (explore),

- the ability to evaluate a design, that is, to recognize opportunities and problems (criteria emergence), and,

- the ability to solve design problems by using past experiences drawn from within or without the current design domain (design adaptation).

When CYCLOPS chooses designs that have some problems, they are passed on to a design adapter, which draws strategies from past design experiences (precedents). The technique that guides the adaptation process is called *demand posting*. This chapter presents the technique.

BACKGROUND

Most design problems are not completely new. Often, parts of a design problem can be solved by reasoning from experience. If one has already seen the problem before, then one has to retrieve the appropriate precedent and apply the earlier solution. If the given problem is new, however, it could be solved by reasoning analogically from a past experience similar to the problem at hand. Further, if the target problem is complex, it can be broken down into subproblems, which in turn, may be solved by reasoning either directly or analogically from precedents.

Solving a design problem by finding matching identical precedents is a fairly well understood task. Analogical matching, on the other hand, is a relatively new research topic in computer aided design. Research interest in this important topic has been growing in recent years, some of the early efforts are: [Mostow 85, Carbonell 86, Gero 87, Ullman & Dietterich 87, Huhns 87, Navinchandra et.al. 87, Goel 89].

An Analogical Reasoning System (ARS) follows a multi-staged process, consisting of the following steps: "**retrieving** a potentially analogous base, **elaborating** the base representation by additional inferences, **mapping** aspects of the base to the target, and **justifying** the mapping" [Kedar-Cabelli 85b]. In order to make an ARS retrieve and apply the appropriate base to the target problem, it has to be given a purpose with which it can search the database of precedents. Several techniques for directing an ARS have been developed. For example, the use of shared goals [Carbonell 83], abstractions [Kolodner 85] and purpose-directed analogy [Kedar-Cabelli 85c].

Finding relevant cases to help adapt a design involves setting up appropriate cues and finding cases that match the cues. We approach these two fundamental tasks using explanation based methods. Our hypothesis is that Case-Based Adaptation for design problems can be controlled through a process of asking relevant questions and modifying the questions based on a causal explanation of the design defect. These questions can then serve as cues into memory [Schank 86]. When a design bug is found, a corresponding question is posed to the Case Knowledge Base (CKB): "Has this, or some similar bug been seen before? Is there a known way of repairing it?"

If a relevant case is not found, the reasons for the bug are used to transform the question. For a given bug X, if related cases are not found, one can ask: What are the causes of X?, If it is not known how to eliminate X, can its causes be eliminated?. This questioning process may be applied recursively until a relevant case is found. I call this technique *dependency tracing*.   Let's consider a simple example: Imagine that you have just built a tree house on the branch of a large tree. Noticing that the branch is sagging too much, you ask yourself: *Can I think of some way of reducing the sagging of the branch?* Assuming no solution comes to mind, the next step is to find the causes of the bug. Two obvious reasons are, that the branch may be too weak, or the tree house may be too heavy. Choosing one of these causes, a new question can be posed: *Is there a way of making the tree house lighter?* This question could lead you to solve the problem by building a smaller tree house.

An interesting outcome of the dependency tracing idea is that better explanations often yield solutions. In the above example, if one had a better understanding of the sagging problem, one might identify one more likely cause of the bug, in addition to the two obvious ones: the cantilever moment arm is too large. A corresponding new question may be posed: *Is there a way of reducing the moment arm?* This question could retrieve a case about how steel ropes are used to reduce the bending of construction cranes. Steel ropes can be similarly used to solve the "sagging-branch" bug. This is a more desirable solution. I believe that the better one's explanation of a bug, the better one's chances of finding a solution. In addition, if one cannot explain a new problem, one cannot solve it.

The idea of asking questions to solve problems has been studied by researchers interested in the psychology of creativity. Osborn's work on Brainstorming [Osborn 53] is particularly relevant. He suggests that problem solving through questioning (self-interrogation) generates remindings which lead to creative ideas.   In his book *Applied Imagination*, he suggests that one of the ways of brainstorming is to redefine the problem question by finding and addressing the causes and effects of the problem[26]. In other words, if you cannot think of a way to solve the given problem directly, try addressing its causes. CYCLOPS implements this question transformation heuristic. An even more comprehensive set of heuristics for problem solving by asking the right questions is presented by Schank in [Schank 86, Schank 88]. It is shown that *tweaking* remindings could yield unexplored questions leading to creative problem solving.

---

[26]The book introduces several other self-interrogation techniques: (1) Can it be put to **other uses**? Are there new ways to use? (2) Can I **adapt**? What else is like this? (3) **Modify**?   New twist? (4) **Magnify**? **Minify**? Longer? Larger? Condensed? (5) **Substitute**? Other ingredients? Other power source? (6) **Redefine**? What are the causes and effects? Can rearrange? (7) Can I **reverse**? Turn upside down? (8) **Combine**? Blend? Alloy?

Given that explanations can be used to generate questions which serve as cues into memory, the next step is to find a way to match these cues with cases. Cases are retrieved by matching the goal (the target) to the case (the base). Matching is done at four levels: directly, by abstraction, by looking up a thesaurus and by analogy. We have examined the first three matching techniques in Chapter 5. We will now examine the fourth and final technique used in CYCLOPS: **Analogical matching**. This technique attempts to match a target problem to a relevant base even if the two have very different surface characteristics [Kedar-Cabelli 85b]. This is done by matching the underlying causal structure of the base and target. This idea draws from the *systematicity-principle* which states that: in order to find an analogical match, between base and target, it is more important to find common causal relationships among attributes in base and target rather than just common attributes [Gentner & Toupin 86]. For design adaptation we have found that, if a case does not directly match the goal (which is to repair a bug), it is possible that one of the subgoals in the case's underlying causal explanation matches the target goal. In this way, a small part of a large case can be relevant to the problem at hand, while the case, taken as a whole, may be irrelevant. This process of *subgoal-matching* has been implemented to match cases and to help focus on relevant portions of cases.

Dependency-tracing and subgoal-matching are used to walk recursively through the causal structures of a case and a target problem (bug), respectively. The combined algorithm is called *Demand Posting*.

EXAMPLE OF CASE BASED DESIGN ADAPTATION

Consider the following design example of siting a house on a steep slope. The problem solving process is composed of the following steps:

1. Problem Recognition. The current state of the designed artifact is posted to the Case Knowledge Base for comments. If any case about a previously encountered bug matches, either directly or through an abstraction, it is retrieved and applied. This is shown in the following scenario:

> *A problem solver is attempting to locate a house on a steep hillside.*
> *It decides to place the house directly on the ground. As soon as it*
> *does this, it is reminded of a situation in which it had placed a*
> *green-colored wooden block on an incline and the block had become*
> *tilted. Its explanation of the situation: The block is tilted because it*

is on a sloped surface. Using this explanation, it infers that the house will also be tilted. It then uses a domain rule to infer that tilted houses are problematic and that this bug needs to be repaired.

2. Explaining the bug. All rules and cases in the system contain fossilized explanations [Kass & Leake 88] which provide the cause of the bug or justify the associated repair strategy. Based on the type of match performed above, the explanation in the case is appropriately modified and copied over to the current bug.

The problem solver finds reasons for the bug by going back to the explanation of the green-block case it used earlier. It explains the house's tilt as being due to two facts: (a) the house is on the ground and, (b) the ground is sloped.

3. Retrieving and Applying a Case. The problem solver first tries to find a case which relates to the bug itself. If such a case is not found, the explanation of the bug is examined to find underlying causes ("sub-bugs"). These new "sub-bugs" are, in effect, sub-goals to the main goal of repairing the bug. In our example, when the program used the block case to recognize that the house will be tilted, it keeps track of the explanation provided in the case.

The problem solver sets up the goal of answering the question: "Is there any way of getting rid of the house's tilt?" Using this goal as a cue, it finds a case about how the ground can be excavated to provide a flat site for the house. Let's assume the problem solver is not satisfied with this solution because it generates new bugs relating to soil erosion. On finding no other relevant case, the problem solver uses the causes of the bug to set up two new disjunctive subgoals: (a) "Is there any way of not having the house on the ground?", or, (b) " Is there any way of making the ground not so steep?". While examining the first sub-goal, the problem solver remembers seeing pictures of village homes in Thailand. The pictures showed huts on stilts. The corresponding explanation was that the villagers, who were having problems with flooding and ground dampness, found a way of getting their homes off the ground: they put their huts on stilts! Drawing from this explanation, the problem solver decides to put its house on stilts too.

4. Looking for other Bugs. As soon as a repair strategy is applied, the system looks for new bugs that might be generated by the repair. In addition, it can also happen that the bug is not completely eliminated and has to be repaired again. Sometimes there may be multiple bugs to solve. In our example, let's assume the problem solver finds a case stating that stilts can be used only if the ground is firm. A new question (*is ground firm*)? is posted to the CKB. The rest of the problem solving process proceeds like this:

> *In order to achieve the sub-goal (is ground firm) the problem solver looks for precedent cases which contain the above sub-goal in their descriptions or explanations. It then finds a case about the use of piles to make landfills strong enough to support buildings. One of the subgoals of using piles is to make the landfill's soil firm. Using this precedent, the problem solver decides to drive piles into the ground. After solving the problem in this way, it re-invokes the process to check if any new problems are generated. If no problems are found, the solution is deemed correct.*

The system follows the above steps recursively to find solutions. In an actual run, the program generates many solutions each of which may involve several repair strategies drawn from different cases. These cases can be from a variety of sources: from the domain of the current design problem (direct match), from a similar domain (abstract match), or from a completely different domain (analogical match). The example illustrates the system's ability to propose solutions based on past experiences instead of relying solely on domain heuristics.

DETAILS ON CASE BASED DESIGN ADAPTATION

Having developed an intuitive understanding of the problem solving process, let us continue by examining the representation used. Cases are represented as observations about the world. An observation has two parts: first, the conditions that existed at the time the observation was made; and second, the consequences (effects) of the observed conditions. For example, while playing with wooden blocks, one might make the observation that: "placing the green-block on a tilted surface causes the block to be tilted." After gaining some experience with blocks, one might develop a better explanation, capturing the fact that the color of the block is irrelevant to the observation. The case is represented as shown in Figure 6-1. Simple clauses capture the conditions and effects of an observation, and include causal links among the clauses. We have found it useful to include explanations of how the effects are caused by the initial conditions as they help focus the case based inference and eliminate unimportant conditional clauses which often tend to distract inference processes.

Precedent#12
conditions: (on block-1 plank-1) and (color block-1 green)
                  and (material block-1 wood) and (is plank-1 sloped)
                  and (is-a plank-1 wooden-plank)
                  and (is-a block-1 toy-block)
effects: (is block-1 tilted)
explanation: (is block-1 tilted) because
                  (on block-1 plank-1) and (is plank-1 sloped)

Figure 6-1: An Explained Observation Case

In addition to basic cases that capture observations, the system also has cases about how different types of design bugs were repaired in the past. These cases are composed of two basic cases, each of which describes an observation. The first part describes the initial problem and the second part describes the solution adopted. The corresponding explanations capture the initial reasons for the existence of the bug and the reasons for the success of the adaptation strategy used. Consider, for example, the case about villagers in Thailand, who put their huts on stilts to avoid flooding problems. Figure 6-2 shows the case as it is represented in CYCLOPS. The precedent has two parts: a situation and a solution. The first part describes the problem and provides an explanation of the problem. The second part describes how the problem was solved. The explanation consists of causal relations among conditions, effects and actions. The relations in the solution part of the precedent represent how subgoals are achieved. The main goal of the precedent is it to achieve: *(not (unfavorable hut "hut is flooded"))* and the subgoals are: *(not (is hut water-logged))* and *(not (on hut ground))*.

Following is a detailed look at the adaptation steps of the example presented in the previous subsection:

1. Problem Recognition. The problem solver recognizes that the house will be tilted and that a tilted house is unfavorable. The problem is recognized using the Green Block case (Figure 6-1), and the If-Then rule shown below:

> **Rule#16**
> **IF:**   (is house tilted)
> **THEN:**   (unfavorable house "tilted house")

The initial conditions of the design are: *(on house site-1) (is site-1 steep)* and *(is-a site-1 site)*. The program matches these conditions to

---

Precedent#10
<u>Initial Situation:</u>
conditions: (on hut ground) ∧ (is ground flooded)
                    ∧ (is hut "in thailand") ∧
effects: (unfavorable hut "hut is flooded")
explanation: (B1) (unfavorable hut "hut is water logged") <u>because</u>
                          (is hut water-logged)
                    (B2) (is hut water-logged) <u>because</u>
                          (on hut ground) <u>and</u> (is ground flooded)
<u>Solution:</u>
action: (action (and (on hut stilts) (on stilts ground)))
effects: (not (unfavorable hut "hut is flooded"))
explanation: (B3) (not (unfavorable hut "hut is flooded")) <u>because</u>
                          (not (is hut water-logged) <u>and</u> (B1) was initially true
                    (B4) (not (is hut water-logged) <u>because</u>
                          (not (on hut ground)) <u>and</u> (B2) was initially true[27]
                    (B5) (not (on hut ground)) <u>because</u>
                          (on hut ground) <u>and</u>
                          the action taken was: (action (and (on hut stilts)
                                                               (on stilts ground)))

Figure 6-2: A precedent case about how villagers in Thailand
put their homes on stilts to guard against floods

---

the precedent and infers that the house will be tilted if it is placed
directly on the steep slope.

The "house" and the "block-1" match by abstraction: They are both
rectangular parallelepipeds as shown in Figure 5-16. "Site-1" and
"plank-1" also match by an abstraction.   The words "steep" and
"sloped" match by a thesaurus lookup.   Following the use of
Precedent#12, the Rule#16 fires and the program infers the clause:
(unfavorable house "tilted house"). Whenever the program infers an
"unfavorable" clause, it treats the clause as a bug that needs to be
repaired. Alternatively, if the user determines that some clause is a
bug, he or she can declare it unfavorable and make the system work on
it.

---

[27]In English, this relation would read as follows: "The hut is not water logged
because it is not on the ground anymore, this is because, the original reason for the hut
being water logged was that it was on ground which was flooded."

2. Explaining the Bug. The causal explanation of a bug is determined from the cases and rules used to infer it. A causal explanation for the bug in our example is shown on the left side of Figure 6-3 Part A. The explanation comes directly from Precedent#12 and Rule#16, and takes the form of a directed acyclic graph with the current bug at the bottom of the the graph.

The right half of the figure shows the adaptation process, which involves asking questions that are generated by tracing dependencies in the causal explanation of the bug. The basic idea is that, if p is caused by q, then $\neg p$ *could* be attained by achieving $\neg q$. The word *could* is used in the last sentence because p might be independently caused by clauses other than q. This problem is corrected during verification. It is important to note that this basic adaptation step works because p is caused by q, the relation is not a logical implication.

As shown in Figure 6-3 Part A, the first question the debugger asks is:

> Q1: Is there some precedent that can achieve:
> *(not (unfavorable house "tilted house"))* ?

Assuming no relevant case is found, the question is transformed by replacing the current problem by its cause. According to the explanation, the cause of *(unfavorable house "tilted house")* is the clause *(is house tilted)*. The new question (Figure 6-3 Part B) reads:

> Q2: Is there some precedent that can achieve: *(not (is house tilted))* ?

Again, assuming no relevant cases are found, let's continue by retrieving the causes of the current problem. According to the explanation, the house is tilted because it is placed on the ground and because the ground is sloped. There are two causes, negating either of the causes should solve the bug. Two new questions (Figure 6-3 Part C) are posted:

> Q3a: Is there some precedent that can achieve:*(not (on house ground))*?

> OR

> Q3b: Is there some precedent that can achieve:*(not (is ground sloped))*?

In the next step, the above questions are used to find relevant cases.

3. Retrieving and Applying a Case. For a given bug, the system looks for cases containing matching goals or sub-goals. The match can be either exact or abstract. Consider, for example, that for some bug p, the clause $\neg p$ has to be achieved. This initiates a search of the case base for any case that "knows" about some clause q that matches $\neg p$ either directly or through an abstraction. A case is said to "know" about q, if the clause q (or $\neg q$) is either its main goal or a subgoal in its underlying causal structure. Next, the causal relations about q are extracted and applied to the bug at hand. The system can encounter two types of causal relations:

1. **$\neg q$ is caused by a set of clauses $\{r,s, t....\}$** . This relation provides a new explanation of the bug p. The relation is spliced into the current explanation. For example, if it is already known that p is caused by $\{l,m,n,....\}$, then p will be said to be caused by either $\{l,m,n,...\}$ or $\{r,s,t,...\}$. The new explanation provides a different "view" of the bug and can lead to some interesting cases.

2. **q is true because some actions $\{a,b,c...\}$ were taken while clauses $\{x,y,z....\}$ were true.** (The set $\{x,y,z,....\}$ typically contains either $\neg q$ or p). This causal relation provides repair actions for achieving $\neg p$. The actions in the relation are spliced onto the developing solution, and the clauses $\{x,y,z,....\}$, which are needed in order to take the repair actions, are treated as new sub-goals to be achieved.

Returning to the example, let us concentrate on question Q3a. The bug is *(on house ground)*. We are trying to achieve the clause *(not (on house ground))*. This clause is used to search the database of cases. Let's assume the program finds a case about how huts in Thailand are put on stilts to protect them from floods. We will examine the case representation before we discuss how and and why the case is retrieved. The case was shown in Figure 6-2. The system retrieves this case because its second subgoal (B5) matches the clause in question (Q3a) above. The matching between the question and the case takes place at a subgoal level. Note that without explanations, the bug could not be transformed into sub-bugs, nor could the case match the current question. Once a match is found between a question and a case, it means that the case "knows" of some way of achieving the matched clause. In the example case, the clause (B5) states that *(not (on hut ground))* is achieved because of the action of putting the hut on stilts and because the hut was originally on the ground. The relation contains an action and a precondition. After matching, this relation is copied over to the evolving solution, as shown in Figure 6-4. The question Q3a is replaced by the action and a new question. The new question Q4: *(on house ground)* is a precondition of the action in the relation (B5). The relation is modified to reflect the new context. The modification is based on the abstract match between the "hut" in the case and the "house" in the current bug. We simply replace one for the other.

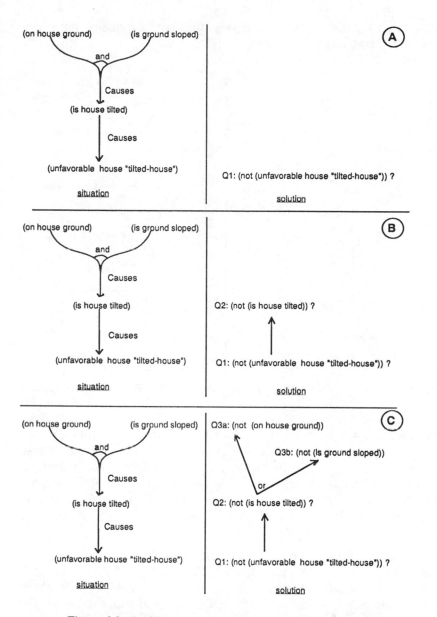

Figure 6-3: Deriving a solution to a given initial "buggy" situation.

As the new question's clause is already true in the initial state and as no other questions remain, the step is complete. In this way, the system solves the original problem of putting a house on a steep slope by putting it on stilts. It has drawn an analogy to a case about flooding to solve a problem about steep slopes. Note that the purpose for which the

stilts were used in the Thai case is very different from the purpose they
serve in the landscape design example.

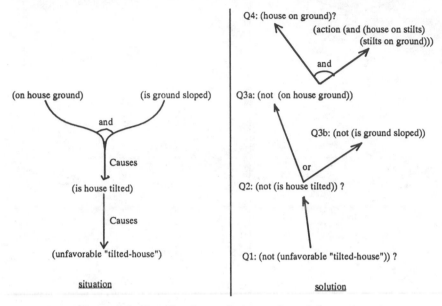

Figure 6-4: Transfer of a repair strategy from the precedent

4. looking for new bugs. Whenever a repair is made, the system
appropriately updates all other inferences made. For example, when it
decides to put the house on stilts, the original fact that the house is on
the ground is not true anymore. Consequently, the green-block case
and the rule used to infer tilt lose support and are retracted. These
operations are performed by an underlying truth maintenance facility.
In addition to retracting decisions as new cases are brought to bear, the
system keeps track of all disjunctive sub-goals. If it fails to find
solutions along one path, it is able to backtrack in order to examine
other paths.

A trace of the system's operation is shown in Figure 6-5. The initial
conditions of the problem are shown in Box **A**. Box **B** shows what the
system infers from the green block case (#12) and the rule about
unfavorable tilted houses (#16). Causal explanations relating the
clauses are also added to the working memory. Boxes **C**, **D**, **E**, and **H**
represent dependency tracing steps. In Box **F**, the system attempts to
solve the bug: *(is ground sloped)* by using a precedent about how
terracing is used to grow rice by stepping mountain sides (Case #9).
Box **G** contains a case based evaluation of the terracing action.
CYCLOPS infers that erosion could become a problem because the

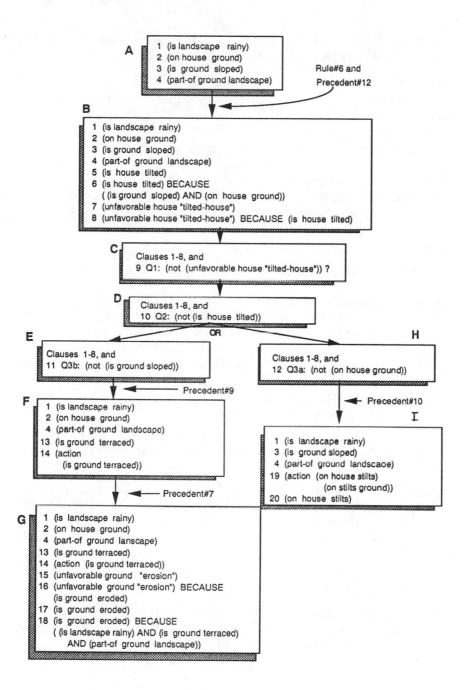

Figure 6-5: A trace of Demand Posting

landscape is rainy. Boxes **H** and **I**, on the other disjunctive branch, shows how the Thailand case (#10) is used in adaptation.

This trace shows how CYCLOPS can:

1. perform truth maintenance functions as bugs are discovered and repaired. For example, note the change in the clauses in Boxes **H** and **I**.
2. pursue multiple disjunctive debugging strategies.
3. use multiple cases to recognize bugs, explain them, take adapting actions, and evaluate solutions.
4. extract adaptation strategies from cases and use them in ways very different from the original use in the case.

NOTES ON DEMAND POSTING

Multiple support for a problem. What happens if a problem has two or more independent causes? When the demand posting algorithm finds a way of eliminating a problem, it "unasserts" the corresponding clause. If there are other independent causes for the clause, the program is fooled into believing that the problem is solved. This situation, however, is only temporary. When CYCLOPS enters the next inference cycle, the problem clause will be re-asserted if there is independent support for it.

Learning. When the demand posting process is used to solve a problem, the resulting situation-solution structure is used as a precedent in future problems.

Completeness assumption for causal relations. The causal relations in a precedent are treated independently. For example, the relation B2 (Figure 6-2) that reads: "the hut is water-logged <u>because</u> the hut is on the ground <u>and</u> the ground is flooded" is a statement that stands alone[28]. However, some relations are dependent on others; for example, B4 is dependent on B2. We assume that a causal relation is complete and that it carries the complete context in its body.

Closed world assumption. CYCLOPS does not actively verify analogies. When an analogy is drawn, the modified design is posted to the precedents data-base. If none of the precedents find a problem, the analogy is deemed correct. We are making the assumption that if a

---

[28]This is similar to the explanations used in XPs [Schank 86]

clause cannot be inferred from the knowledge possessed, then it is false. This is a closed world assumption on the knowledge base.

Indexing many precedents. Based on the completeness assumption, all the causal relations of all the precedents are indexed independently. The index is based on the clauses that the relations assert. We currently use a flat indexing mechanism, only because it serves our immediate needs. For large databases, a discrimination-network based technique could be used for indexing [Kolodner 80].

SUMMARY

One of the characteristics of an innovative design system is its ability to use precedents to solve design problems. Problems can be solved by reasoning analogically from precedents retrieved from long term memory. Retrieving a precedent, among other things, requires providing the Analogical Reasoning System (ARS) with a purpose. In this chapter we examined a technique, *demand posting*, that is used to post questions to a database of previous designs.

In a demand posting system, whenever a problem is detected a demand is posted to the case base, requesting a precedent that can solve the problem. If an appropriate precedent is not found, the causes of the problem are retrieved and new demands are posted. This process continues recursively till a solution is found. If not, the attempt to adapt the design is abandoned.

The demand posting technique consists of two parts: Dependency Tracking and Subgoal Matching:

Dependency-tracking involves the following steps: first, the problem is identified; second, the problem statement is posted as a demand on the database of precedents. This means that the database manager has to find precedents that match the demand (pattern).

If no suitable precedent is found, the program retrieves the causes of the problem. These causes are then posted as demands. This process of posting demands, retrieving causes of problems and posting the causes as new demands proceeds recursively till "suitable" precedents are found, or the attempt to adapt the design is abandoned.

Subgoal-matching. A precedent is said to be "suitable" with respect to a posted demand (pattern) if it contains a design strategy which attains a goal (pattern) that matches the demand. If such a match is found, the design strategy in the precedent is transferred to the current design problem. If, on the other hand, a match between the demand and the goal of the precedent is not found, the program retrieves a pre-coded explanation of how the design strategy in the precedent attains the precedent's goal. An explanation is usually a trace of how the different parts of the overall strategy address the subgoals of the overall goal. After retrieving an explanation, the program compares the demand (pattern) with the subgoals of the precedent strategy in order to find a match. If no match is found, failure is announced.

This technique can match a base and target even if their main goals or surface features are radically different. It is for this reason that the program appears to reason analogically. The demand posting technique is fairly general and could be extended to use strategies other than dependency tracking. This could lead to systems that could serve as brainstorming assistants to designers.

Chapter 7
Putting It All Together: A Detailed Architecture of CYCLOPS

In this chapter we will see how the techniques described in the last four chapters fit into one coherent system. Recall that in Chapter 1 we introduced the program's architecture in a simplified form (Figure 1-4, Page 14), we will now take a detailed look at it.

CYCLOPS' architecture can be viewed in three layers, each representing the program's operating modes: the *normal search* mode, the *exploration* mode and the *adaptation* mode.

NORMAL SEARCH MODE

In the normal search mode, the program performs the *PO-A** algorithm (Chapter 4) to find all non-dominated solutions, provided they exist. This is shown in Part-I of Figure 7-1. The search process uses two modules: a *synthesizer*, and a *selector*. The synthesizer takes partial designs and adds detail to them by instantiating their variables. The selector checks for dominance and places the designs in either a dormant or an active list. The active designs constitute the non-dominated set and are returned to the search process.

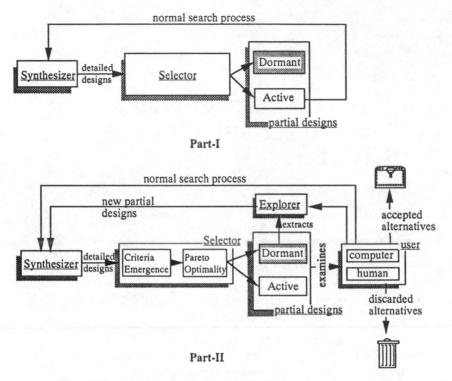

Figure 7-1: Normal search mode (Part-I), Exploration mode (Part-II)

EXPLORATION MODE

In the exploration mode, CYCLOPS relaxes the governing criteria and searches alternatives outside the original solution space using the $OPO\text{-}A^*$ algorithm. This is done by the *explorer* module (Part-II of Figure 7-1). The explorer examines designs that have been discarded by the selector. It tries to see if there are potential opportunities in the designs that have been dominated. This is done by emerging new criteria during design. The *selector* has a *criteria emergence* submodule that matches design alternatives against precedents (this aspect is shown in the complete architecture, Figure 7-2).

The *user* plays an important role during exploration. The user examines designs and decides to either accept or discard them. If the user accepts a complete design, it is stored in the treasure chest. If it is incomplete, it is put back into the normal search process. The user can either be human or a program or a team of both.

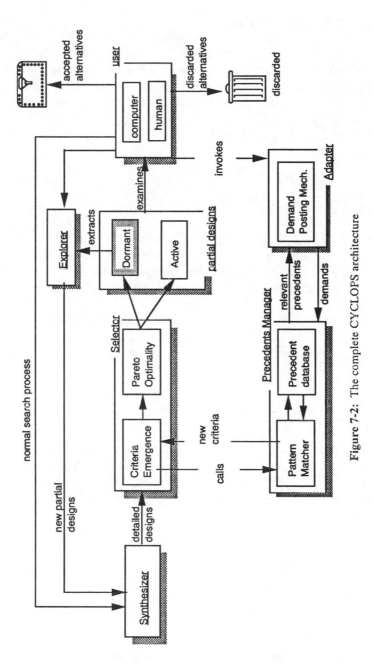

Figure 7-2: The complete CYCLOPS architecture

ADAPTATION MODE

In the adaptation mode, CYCLOPS uses precedent knowledge to solve design problems. The *adapter* runs the demand posting algorithm. It posts demands on the precedents manager and accepts precedents to draw analogies from. As described above, the precedents manager is also used by the *selector* module. Just before the selector applies a dominance check (*pareto optimality*), it checks designs for problems or opportunities.

OPERATING CYCLOPS

CYCLOPS is started by putting the root node in the "active" box. The program starts in the normal search mode. If no solutions are found, or if the user makes a request, the program goes into the exploration mode. The adapter is invoked only by the user. This is done because, adaptation is computationally expensive and hence it is not possible to try and adapt each and every design produced by the synthesizer.

A trace of one of the implementations of CYCLOPS is provided in Appendix B.

THE IMPLEMENTATION

CYCLOPS is implemented in FranzLisp[29] and runs on VAX[30] machines running the UNIX[31] operating system. CYCLOPS' interface uses the X[32] window system. The program has 20 precedents and has been run on problems with 10 landuses and 15 lots.

---

[29]Trademark of Franz Inc., Alameda, CA

[30]Trademark of Digital Equipment Corp, Maynard, MA

[31]AT&T Bell Labs, NJ

[32]Developed at MIT's Project Athena

Chapter 8
Relationship to Other Work

In this chapter we will compare the techniques used in CYCLOPS to those of other systems. Readers who wish to get a broader sense of the techniques used in Design Automation (DA) systems may refer to the following papers [Mostow 85, Sriram 86, Tong 86, Navinchandra 90].

In the course of the book we have seen how:

- some design problems can be represented as *multi-criteria, configuration* problems, and how search can be used to solve such problems;

- innovative designs can be generated by *exploring* a wide range of alternatives;

- precedents can be used to *adapt* designs which have problems.

The chapter has three parts. The first is about optimization in configuration problems. We will relate CYCLOPS to other work in OR and AI-based design automation. The second part relates CYCLOPS' exploratory behavior to AI-based discovery systems. The third part discusses precedent-based reasoning and the origins of the demand posting algorithm.

DESIGN AS A MULTI-CRITERIA CONFIGURATION PROBLEM

Several conceptual design problems can be viewed as *configuration* tasks. Many of the AI-based design automation systems solve conceptual design problems using search and *constraint-satisfaction* techniques. Although these systems use different problem solving techniques, a majority of them treat design as a satisficing problem and assume that a solution space always exists. CYCLOPS builds on the ideas in these systems by requiring *multi-criteria* optimization in addition to consistency over constraints. Multi-criteria situations often tend to be over-constrained requiring our system to have the ability to *relax criteria* and recognize critical *tradeoffs*.

Constraint satisfaction and Configuration Problems.

The work on constraint manipulation and satisfaction includes these techniques: generate and test [Buchanan & Feigenbaum 78, Lindsay 80]; network consistency algorithms [Mackworth 77]; combined backtracking and constraint-based reasoning [Fikes 70]; dependency directed backtracking [Stallman & Sussman 77]; the constraint posting idea [Stefik 80]; and forward-checking in consistent labeling problems [Nadel 85d].

Our decision to view landscape design as a configuration task is motivated by some of the early work on design automation. In particular AIR-CYL [Brown & Chandrasekaran 86] and PRIDE [Mittal 85]. Both these systems use a combination of design goals and constraints to guide the solution process. PRIDE views its task of designing paper transports for photocopiers as a configuration task involving the choice and location of paper handling mechanisms such as rolling-stations, pinch-rolls and paper-guides. Similarly, CYCLOPS views landscape design as a spatial configuration of landuses such as houses, churches and schools. CYCLOPS differs from the majority of other conceptual design automation systems in that it requires designs to be optimal.

There are several techniques for multi-objective optimization [Goicoechea 82]. These deal with continuous, monotonic functions and thus cannot be applied to landscape design problems. This is because landscape problems can have criteria that are non-linear, non-monotonic, non-continuous and discrete. Such problems can be solved is only by heuristic search. Finding optimal solutions using search involves *look ahead*. Further, finding solutions over multiple objectives almost always involves making *tradeoffs*.

Look ahead.   Optimization by searching requires some method for "looking ahead".   The technique used in CYCLOPS is based on the notion of admissibility [Hart, Nilsson & Raphael 68].   The A^* algorithm is modified to handle multiple-criteria, using dominance as a measure of optimality. CYCLOPS achieves admissibility by choosing optimistic values from previously enumerated tables of possible outcomes. The program estimates the "cost to completion" of partial designs by making optimistic assumptions about how the rest of the design will be completed. Other approaches to looking ahead include: the use of abstract operators for VLSI design in the DONTE system [Tong 88]; use of micro-structural properties of alloys as rough designs in the alloy design program ALADIN [Rychner et.al. 86]; and use of rough parameter values in AIR-CYL [Brown & Chandrasekaran 86]. These systems, unlike CYCLOPS, do not look for globally optimal solutions.

Tradeoffs. In multi-criteria problems, the solution space often tends to be over constrained. Criteria have to be relaxed and traded off against one another in order to find solutions. CYCLOPS handles this problem by using a representation for constraints and objectives that allows for relaxations when required.   The program, however, leaves all final tradeoff decisions in the hands of the user. Some systems, on the other hand, have explicit tradeoff heuristics.   For example, the two VLSI design systems VEXED [Steinberg 87] and ULYSSES [Bushnell & Director 86] have explicit rules such as: "IF the goal is to minimize delay of an adder circuit, THEN prefer carry-lookahead over ripple-carry".   CYCLOPS does not use explicit knowledge to prefer one design decision over another.

DESIGN EXPLORATION

As we have noted, innovative designs are not obtained through some deliberate attempt at producing them, but by generating lots of designs and by throwing away the bad ones. Consequently, the ability of a system to innovate depends on how well it can generate diverse alternatives that break away from the norms and the governing constraints.   The idea is that new alternatives can sometimes *serendipitously* lead to interesting solutions.

The idea of exploration was inspired by Darwin's theory of evolution. In his book *On the Origin of Species* he notes:

"As many more individuals of each species are born than can

> possibly survive; and as, consequently, there is a frequently
> recurring struggle for existence, it follows that any being, if it
> varies however slightly in any manner profitable to itself,
> under the complicated and sometimes varying condition of
> life, will have a better chance of surviving, and thus be
> naturally selected."   - **Charles Darwin** [Darwin 59].

Restating the quotation, for the design domain, we get:

> As many more designs are generated than can possibly
> survive pruning; and as, consequently, there is a frequently
> recurring test of optimality, it follows that any design, if it
> varies however slightly in any manner profitable to itself or
> its variations, under the complex and sometimes varying set
> of constraints and objectives, will (together with its
> variations) have a better chance of surviving the pruning test,
> and thus be naturally selected.

CYCLOPS explores alternatives (variations) by relaxing criteria; it tests
for optimality by selecting non-dominated alternatives. In addition, it
discovers opportunities by reasoning from a database of past
experiences.

Several systems that discover solutions by exploring the state space, for
example: DENDRAL, a program that searches for novel structural
combinations of organic molecules [Buchanan & Feigenbaum 78];
DALTON, a system that discovers molecular compositions based on
given reactions [Langley et.al. 87]; SIDS, a bridge design system that
discovers novel combinations of structural elements [Cheyayeb 87];
EDISON, a program that invents new mechanical systems [Dyer et.al.
86]; BACON, a quantitative discovery system that finds relations
among variables; and AM, a system that discovers new mathematical
concepts [Lenat 76].

All the systems cited above are based on the idea of searching the state
space using special heuristics. As the state space tends to be very large,
it is important to control the combinatorics with good exploration
techniques.   Examples of the techniques are: use of chemical
knowledge in DENDRAL's generator; DALTON's use of domain
knowledge such as laws of conservation and combining volumes to
limit the search; BACON's use of quantitative heuristics such as
inversion and multiplication ; and AM's use of mutations. The
exploration technique used in CYCLOPS is criteria relaxation. The
program explores new alternatives outside the solution space by
relaxing the criteria that bound the space.

Other approaches to exploration are based on making changes directly
to the artifact being generated.   For example, AM explores new

mathematical concepts by applying mutation operators to the LISP code that represents simple mathematical concepts. Similarly, EDISON invents new mechanical systems by making mutations to the artifacts it deals with [Dyer et.al. 86]. For example, it might take a door and chop it in half to discover a bar-room door, or it might randomly rearrange the hinges to produce a trap door. CYCLOPS, on the other hand, does not make mutations directly to the artifact but to the constraints and objectives that bound the artifact solution space. This is done because applying mutators directly to the artifacts can produce too many useless alternatives [Lenat 84]. In CYCLOPS criteria relaxations are gradual; we only look at those alternatives which are barely dominated. This allows us to gradually move away from the solution space every time a relaxation is made. It should be noted that although this technique, at first, looks only at solutions close to each other on the pareto graph, it can generate artifacts that have very different physical characteristics. Just because two solutions are close to each other on the pareto graph does not mean they are structurally similar. Mutation operators, on the other hand, can only generate solutions that are structurally close; if the mutations are too radical they run the risk of producing too much junk. In CYCLOPS, we saw how a threshold-based[33] algorithm $(OPO\text{-}A^*)$ can be used to explore the artifact space by making relaxations in the criteria space.

Another way CYCLOPS is different from the other systems is that it can extend the search space dynamically. This happens when CYCLOPS uses new objects drawn from precedents. For example, we saw how CYCLOPS used stilts to solve a design problem. The notion of stilts was not in the original representation and came from outside it. A program's ability to opportunistically extend the state space is very useful. The idea is not to start the search process using a fully extended state space, but to extend it as required.

In order to innovate, it is important not only to be able to explore new alternatives but also to be able to recognize innovative alternatives when they are generated. The BACON program, for example, discovers new laws by detecting numerical trends. Using a depth-first control strategy, the program generates data that is checked for patterns and relationships among variables. The AM system uses heuristics of "interestingness" to move from one interesting concept to another. For example, AM considers extreme cases of set membership interesting; a

---

[33]Our use of thresholds is similar to those used in the ID-A* algorithm [Korf 85]. However, our purpose for using thresholds is completely different.

prime number is interesting because it belongs to a set of numbers that have no divisors other than itself and unity. In the same spirit, CYCLOPS also recognizes interesting designs, but its mechanism is based on past experiences (precedents). If CYCLOPS finds a design to be interesting for some reason, it introduces a corresponding new criterion. CYCLOPS emerges new criteria by matching design alternatives against precedents. The idea is not to start with a long list of criteria in the beginning of the search, but to add new ones as when they become relevant.

The criteria emergence idea is somewhat similar, in spirit, to the serendipity recognition mechanism in the DAYDREAMER system [Muller 87]. DAYDREAMER takes descriptions of events in the world as input and produces a sequence of events it will perform in an imaginary (dream) world. The program plans its dreams by performing an intersection search in a network of rules. In order to find serendipity in a given state, it starts by finding a rule that corresponds to the state. It then tries to find a path between the state and its goals using intersection search. If it finds a connection, a serendipity is recognized.

DESIGN ADAPTATION

Because innovation, in a given design domain, comes from the ability to use knowledge drawn from inside or outside the current domain, an innovative design system should be able to draw *analogies* between its target problem and base precedents drawn from a varied set of sources. In addition, the system should have some way of knowing which precedents it should use. It cannot try to draw analogies from all precedents in memory; a context-dependent method for *retrieval* is required.

CYCLOPS' *demand posting* technique for adapting designs by drawing analogies to previous cases, is motivated by Osborn's work on Brainstorming [Osborn 53]. Its subgoal matching technique draws directly from the Structure Mapping Principle [Gentner 83, Gentner & Toupin 86] and Winston's idea of matching and transferring causal structure from base to target [Winston 80, Winston et.al. 83]. Subgoal matching is based on using the causal structure (explanations) of precedents to find analogies without being distracted by irrelevant features in the base precedent. This is done using a representation which captures the goals and sub-goals of the prior design, linked by causal relationships. Goel, in the KRITIK system, has proposed a model-based representation capturing structural and behavioral interactions, together with the internal causal behaviors of the design [Goel 89, Goel & Chandrasekaran 89]. This approach represents the state of final design and its behavior, while in CYCLOPS' cases contain the process of how the final design was arrived at; a design-record capturing the conditions before and after a problem solving step is taken. In CYCLOPS, the problem solving steps of a prior case are re-used, not the prior design itself.

Design adaptation, in addition to *demand posting*, can also be achieved by finding modifications through analysis. Two systems that take this approach are PROMPT [Murthy & Addanki 87] and 1stPRINCE [Cagan 88]. The PROMPT system debugs designs by performing a qualitative analysis of the problem. It uses modification operators which are either drawn from a pre-defined set or derived by analyzing the governing equations. PROMPT adapts by reasoning from first principles, CYCLOPS adapts by reasoning from past experiences. These approaches could complement each other.

Precedent Retrieval by Asking Questions

Techniques such as Brainstorming [Osborn 53] and Synectics [Gordon 61] are aimed at helping people be creative by inducing them to take different views of a problem and by drawing interesting analogies. In order to make such analogies, one needs to retrieve the right precedents, which, in turn, is accomplished by asking the right questions. Several techniques for posing questions have been developed: Wishful and fanciful thinking [Rickards 74]; boundary examinations [Rickards 74]; Brainstorming; Synectics; Divergent Thinking [Guilford 59]; and Ideonomy (Wall St. Journal, June 1, 1987). CYCLOPS implements one of the brainstorming techniques in its demand posting algorithm.

Two other systems use question transformation to retrieve episodes: CYRUS [Kolodner 81] and SWALE [Schank 86]. CYRUS is a question answering program that uses domain knowledge to transform given questions as needed. CYRUS can convert a seemingly unanswerable question into a series of questions that are relevant to the data in its episodic memory. SWALE is an understanding system that creatively retrieves and uses precedents. Given a story, the program starts by checking to see if the story is consistent with memory. If not, it retrieves episodes from memory and tweaks them to help explain the inconsistency. In his book *Explanation Patterns*, Schank provides a long list of heuristics that can be used for question transformation and episode tweaking. All these heuristics have not been incorporated in SWALE yet. CYCLOPS does one kind of question transformation and does not tweak precedents explicitly.

CONCLUSIONS

CYCLOPS draws ideas from several research efforts in different disciplines. Many of the systems cited in the chapter seem unrelated to one-another when taken independently, but not when studied in the context of design. Design is a complex enough activity which involves a wide range of human faculties and problem solving activities. Future research in design will draw ideas from an even wider range of disciplines and will serve as a forum for integrating diverse ideas.

Chapter 9
Assumptions, Shortcomings, and Future Research

CYCLOPS' approach makes several assumptions and its current implementation has several shortcomings. In the future, a list of issues will have to be tackled, among them are:

Hierarchical approach. CYCLOPS views designs as consistent labeling problems. The representation is flat and and all at one level of detail, making it very difficult to tackle large problems. If a landscape problem which required locating a hundred houses on a large landscape, the combinatorial explosion could grind any computer down to a halt. On the other hand, if we divided the hundred houses into clusters and grouped clusters into neighborhoods, we could design at different levels of abstraction. One of the biggest challenges in developing a hierarchical algorithm for Consistent Labeling Optimization Problems is to find some way of assuring non-dominance of generated solutions; a non-dominated solution at one level of abstraction is not guaranteed to remain non-dominated at lower levels of abstraction.

Exploiting commonalities. When CYCLOPS produces design alternatives, it checks them for opportunities and tries to adapt designs which have bugs. Unfortunately, only a very small percentage of the generated alternatives turn out to be interesting, and consequently, a lot of time and effort gets wasted. One obvious way of alleviating the problem is to have CYCLOPS examine alternatives in parallel. This approach would improve performance to some extent. The real problem, however, is more subtle. Many of the alternatives generated by the program have common features, making it unnecessary for the system to examine all the alternatives in full detail. As CYCLOPS does not look for commonalities, it repeatedly discovers the same opportunity in several designs, expending the same amount of effort each time. There are two ways to approach this problem: (a) the program could be modified to learn as it examines designs. It could remember its findings and use them in the future, and thus, avoid duplication of effort or, (b) the program could examine the designs to identify common problems and solve the problems only once. We feel that the second approach is better; as the first will require too much memory. We need some way of identifying commonalities and solving them at a level of abstraction higher than the individual designs. An added advantage of this approach is improved user interaction. CYCLOPS currently requires users to make tradeoffs among individual designs - a slow process. It would be better if the program extracted commonalities and had the user make tradeoffs at higher levels of abstraction before examining individual designs.

Flat Indexing. CYCLOPS indexes all precedents on the patterns that correspond to their goals and sub-goals in the precedents. These are stored in a flat database, requiring excessive search whenever a precedent is requested. A network based indexing could help alleviate this problem [Kolodner 80]. Further, we would like the indexing scheme to change in response to new information and new problem solving contexts. In other words, we would like the memory organization to be dynamic [Schank 82]. One of the major problems is coming up with a dynamic indexing scheme that can index not only on the attributes of the precedents but also on the relationships among attributes. This would allow *systematicity*-based access to the precedent database.

Causal and Functional Demand Posting. CYCLOPS adapts designs by tracking the causal dependencies of design problems. It is possible to expand this framework to deal with design functions. A technique called functional demand posting could be developed to solve design problems by tracking design functions and sub-functions. Consequently, a design process may be allowed to switch between causal and functional demand posting as and when required.

FUTURE APPLICATIONS

Applications to other Consistent Labeling Optimization Problems.
The CLOP is a fairly general formulation and is applicable to a large
range of problems. For example:

- <u>Site Planning.</u> All constraint-based layout problems can be
  formulated as CLPs.

- <u>Scheduling.</u> In a job-shop situation one has to decide which
  job, goes where, on which machine, undergoes which
  operation and at what time period. Each schedule attribute
  can be treated as a variable in a CLP formulation. Criteria
  may include items such as resource availability, due dates,
  cost minimization, idle-time minimization etc.

- <u>Facilities Maintenance Management</u>. A building facility
  deteriorates over time. In coming up with a maintenance
  strategy one has to decide, when to maintain, what
  maintenance action to take, how often and what level of
  serviceability is acceptable. As the problem often involves
  non-linear,   non-monotonic   functions,   standard
  mathematical programming techniques are not appropriate.
  A CLOP algorithm could be used to find optimal values for
  the decision variables.

Exploring Alternatives in a Decision Support System. CYCLOPS
can generate alternatives and identify critical tradeoffs. If the program
were used in a decision support environment, it could help decision
makers play what-if games or locate critical tradeoffs in complex multi-
attribute situations.

Learning to design by Discovery. A design that is adapted by
CYCLOPS is represented in the same way as the precedents it uses.
Consequently, each adaptation that CYCLOPS performs can be used as
a precedent in future design problems. This capability has not been
implemented yet. However, if the problem of precedent indexing and
generalization is solved, one could use CYCLOPS to discover designs
by setting it off on an unsupervised exploration.

CONTRIBUTIONS

The concepts presented in this book draw on ideas from several disciplines and, consequently, make contributions to many of them:

Engineering Optimization. The Consistent Labeling Optimization Problem Solving methodology (CLOPS) is an interactive, multi-attribute decision making (MADM) technique. As CLOPS uses a branch and bound technique, it allows for evaluation of partial solutions during the solution process. This makes CLOPS more efficient than traditional MADM techniques which generate complete solutions before testing them. Further, as CLOPS works in discrete spaces, it can handle constraints and objectives that are non-monotonic, non-linear or non-continuous. The CLOPS methodology is applicable to a large number of engineering optimization problems that cannot be solved by standard mathematical programming techniques.

Artificial Intelligence. The demand posting technique is interesting for its ability to employ multiple precedents or parts of precedents to solve a problem either directly or analogically. It provides a technique for indexing into memory by posting demands and reformulating those demands when appropriate precedents are not found.

Design Automation/Computer-Aided Design. The idea of exploring design alternatives by criteria relaxation is a new one. It offers designers a way of identifying critical tradeoffs and promising alternatives. Further, the use of precedents-based reasoning in design is a relatively new idea [Mostow 85]. We have developed a method for representing precedents that simultaneously allows for problem identification, criteria emergence, and analogical problem solving.

Epilogue

In order to innovate, one must have an open mind. One must be willing to relax one's constraints in order to examine alternatives. Innovation comes from one's ability to break the rules, to look beyond the norms and to avoid mind-sets. In fact, many of the ideas about constraint relaxation presented in this book are themselves a result of constraint relaxation! As I recall, the hardest task in applying constraint relaxation to a problem is not the relaxation of the constraints but their identification in the first place. We often solve problems making too many assumptions about the world. Our training forces us to impose constraints without being aware of them. For example, consider the following question: "Why do flat mirrors flip images left to right and not up to down?". Many people have problems answering this question, as they make assumptions about mirrors that are really not necessary. Computer models such as CYCLOPS can handle constraints that are explicit in the representation. People, however, can solve problems by extending or changing their view of the problem by switching among representations. We have yet to understand this process.

We argued that relaxing constraints and taking different views of a problem can make us recall experiences that help in solving problems. The question is, can a computer contribute to this process? Can computers be creativity tools? I believe we can build innovative design tools that will serve as brainstorming assistants. Such programs would work from a large databank of precedents drawn from many different fields.

Innovation is not as mysterious as it is made out to be. We are now beginning to understand some of its underlying processes. We have uncovered some components of those processes which can now be incorporated in computer programs. It will be a long time before we will realize all our goals, but current technology is at a stage where useful creativity tools can indeed be developed. This is only a beginning.

Appendix A
The Consistent Labeling Optimization Problem

In this appendix we will take a formal look at the *PO-A** and *OPO-A** algorithms. We will review other techniques and see how the *PO-A** algorithm is developed.

The appendix starts with a formulation of the Consistent Labeling Optimization Problem, followed by a description of a CLP algorithm called Forward Checking [Nadel 85a]. After describing the CLP algorithm, a new algorithm for CLOPs is developed. Finally a proof of optimality of the CLOP algorithm is provided.

INTRODUCTION

Over the past decade, the consistent labeling problem has received considerable interest in Artificial Intelligence. In particular, machine vision, cryptography and theorem proving. Many algorithms have been developed for solving consistent labeling problems. A majority of these algorithms are based on heuristic search. Techniques such as constraint propagation and forward checking have been used to reduce search effort.

In general, a CLP is formulated thus: (Adapted from [Nadel 85a])

1. There is a set of variables.

2. Each variable has associated with it, a finite set of values. These sets are known as the domains of the variables.

3. There is a set of constraints on the values that various combinations of variables may compatibly take on, and

4. The goal is to find a few (or all) ways to assign to each

variable, a value from its associated domain in such a way that all constraints are simultaneously satisfied.

The consistent labeling problem places few requirements on the nature of the variables or the constraints: the constraints can be either symbolic or numeric, monotonic or non-monotonic, continuous or discontinuous, linear or non-linear.

FORMULATING THE CONSISTENT LABELING OPTIMIZATION PROBLEM

The consistent labeling optimization problem is a modified CLP with an added requirement; generating labelings that are optimal over a given set of objectives. The problem formulation used in this chapter is based on the notation introduced by Nadel [Nadel 85a, Nadel 85b]. A CLOP has four basic components: variables, values, constraints, and objectives.

Variables

The CLOP handles discrete variables only. Let Z be a set of n such variables, where $Z = \{ z_1, z_2, \cdots z_n \}$ and $n \in \{2,3,4 \cdots \}$.

Values

Each variable has associated with it, a set of possible values it can take. The set associated with the variable z_i is denoted by d_{z_i} and is called the domain (or range) of the variable. The set of domains, $\mathbf{d} = \{ d_{z_1}, d_{z_2} \cdots d_{z_n} \}$ is prespecified.

Constraints

The set of constraints is denoted by C. A given constraint c_j constrains a set of variables Z_j where, $Z_j \subseteq Z$. The constraint is a relation among the variables in Z_j. This relation is denoted by T_j. This means that T_j is the set of consistent labelings taken from all possible labelings of the variables in Z_j.

In other words, $T_j \subseteq D_j$ where, $D_j = \bigtimes_{z_i \in Z_j} [d_{z_i}]$, the set of all possible labelings of Z_j.

A constraint has a corresponding function called its Constraint Function (CF_j). The arguments to the constraint function is a labeling of the variables in Z_j. Any such arbitrary labeling of Z_j is denoted by $\overline{Z}_j$. The function call $CF_j(\overline{Z}_j)$ returns a value of either 1 or N, where N is some very large number $\to \infty$. Consequently, any $\overline{Z}_j$ with $CF_j(\overline{Z}_j) = 1$ is said to be a consistent labeling on Z_j with respect to c_j. Hence:

$$T_j = \{\overline{Z}_j \in D_j | CF_j(\overline{Z}_j) = 1 \} \qquad \text{(A.1)}$$

In other words, T_j is the set of $\overline{Z}_j$ that satisfy constraint c_j.

Let us now look at an example of the formulation we have this far. This example will be used to illustrate points throughout the appendix. (All references to the example will appear between two horizontal lines as shown below.)

Example

Assume there are three variables (n = 3): $Z = \{z_1 z_2 z_3\}$ with domains {1 2}, {1 2 3} and {a b} respectively. There are three constraints c_1 c_2 and c_3. The three constraints are shown below:

<u>Constraint</u> c_1 has CF_1 : $(2z_1)^2 + z_2^2 \geq 18$

As c_1 constrains z_1 & z_2, the range of the constraint is $Z_1 = \{z_1, z_2\}$. Given the domains of z_1 and z_2, the value of the function can be calculated in tabular form:

actual	z2 = 1	z2 = 2	z2 = 3
z1 = 1	5	8	13
z1 = 2	17	20	25

The table is converted into CF values based on CF_1:

CF_1	z2 = 1	z2 = 2	z2 = 3
z1 = 1	N	N	N
z1 = 2	N	1	1

The CF_j returns values from the CF values table shown above. Boxes with value 1 satisfy the given constraint, while boxes with the letter N are inconsistent. For example, the labeling $\overline{Z}_j = \{1\ 2\}$ has $CF = N$ and is thus inconsistent. The set of legal labelings for $c_1 = T_1 = \{(2\ 2)(2\ 3)\}$.

<u>Constraint</u> c_2 has CF_2: $10e^{0.1z_1z_2} \geq 13$
Actual values:

actual	z2 = 1	z2 = 2	z2 = 3
z1 = 1	11	12	13
z1 = 2	12	15	25

CF values:

CF_2	z2 = 1	z2 = 2	z2 = 3
z1 = 1	N	N	1
z1 = 2	N	1	1

<u>Constraint</u> c_3 is non-numeric and has CF_3 expressed directly as a CF table:

CF_3	z2 = 1	z2 = 2	z2 = 3
z3 = a	N	1	N
z3 = b	1	N	N

Objectives

The set of objectives is denoted by $O=\{o_1, o_2 \cdots o_3\}$. A particular objective o_h has a set of variables that it contains: Z_h. Where $Z_h \subseteq Z$. The objective is characterized by a relation T_h on the variables in Z_h. Which means that T_h is the set of optimal labelings taken from D_h where $D_h = \mathsf{X}_{z_i \in Z_h} [d_{z_i}]$, the set of all possible labelings of Z_h. Objectives are represented in the same way as constraints[34]. The relation imposed by an objective on D_h is similar to that of a constraint, in that, T_h is *constrained* to be optimal.

Example

For now, let's assume there is one objective, o_4 in our example:

Objective o_4 has CF_4: Maximize $Sine(40z_1+z_2)$. The corresponding actual value and CF value tables are:

---

[34]We will relax this definition later.

Actual Values:

actual	z2 = 1	z2 = 2	z2 = 3
z1 = 1	.72	.72	.73
z1 = 2	.99	.99	.99

CF values:

CF_4	z2 = 1	z2 = 2	z2 = 3
z1 = 1	N	N	N
z1 = 2	1	1	1

A Characterization of T_j and T

Let $\overline{Z}$ denote any arbitrary labeling of the variables in Z. $\overline{Z}$ is a set of values for each variable z_i chosen from the variable's respective domain. Any n-tuple $\overline{Z} \in D = \underset{z_i \in z}{\mathsf{X}} d_{z_i}$ can be either consistent or not.

For a labeling $\overline{Z}$ to be consistent it should return value 1 from the Constraint Functions of all the constraints and objectives. This is done by looping through all the CFs and passing them the right arguments taken from $\overline{Z}$. For example, if $\overline{Z} = \{\overline{z}_1, \overline{z}_2, \overline{z}_3, \overline{z}_4\}$ and Z_j of $c_j = \{z_2, z_4\}$ then we have to extract the second and fourth values from $\overline{Z}$ to serve as inputs to CF_j. This action is denoted by $\overline{Z}_j \langle \overline{Z} \rangle$, which is called the projection of $\overline{Z}$ onto $\overline{Z}_j$. In our example, $\overline{Z}_j \langle \overline{Z} \rangle = \{\overline{z}_2, \overline{z}_4\}$.

Consequently, the global set of consistent labelings T is given by:

$$T = \{\overline{Z} \mid \overline{Z} \in D \wedge \overline{Z}_j \langle \overline{Z} \rangle \in T_j \quad \forall_{j \in J_1^c}\} \tag{A.2}$$

Where, c is the total number of constraints (m) and objectives (h) and is given by: $c = (m + h)$. J_1^c is the set of all integers from 1 to c, the total number of CFs in the CLOP.

SOLVING CLPS WITH THE FORWARD CHECKING ALGORITHM

Before describing how a CLOPS is solved we will first review a technique for solving CLPs. The technique is called Forward Checking and was suggested by Haralick and Elliot [Haralick and Elliot 80]. The notation used here is from Nadel [Nadel 85d].

We must first define the terms we will be using to perform and characterize the search for consistent labelings. For the sake of simplicity, it is assumed that the variables in Z are instantiated in numerical order. (The problem of finding a suitable instantiation ordering is in itself an NP-complete problem and is not examined here.)

Searching the State Space

Let X denote the global instantiation order of the variables in Z, where $X=\{x_1,x_2,\cdots x_n\}$ (which we assume to be the same order as in Z). This could, however, be any random order, as there are **n!** possible orderings.

The search process starts by instantiating the variables in the order $x_1,x_2,\cdots$ till x_n. Each instantiation corresponds to a stage in the search tree. The stage number is denoted by k. The variables that have been instantiated at stage k are denoted by X_k, which is given by:

$$X_k = \{x_1,x_2,\cdots x_k\} \tag{A.3}$$

The variables in Z that have yet to be instantiated are called *Future Variables* and are denoted by F_k. The search progresses from stage to stage by concatenating the domains of variables to partial labelings generated by the previous stages. This is denoted by a concatenation operator: $\parallel$. For example, if there is a list $A = (abcdef)$, then $A \parallel q$ gives the new list $(abcdefq)$.

Correspondingly, $\overline{X}_k = \overline{X}_{k-1} \parallel d_{\overline{x}_k}$. Where $d_{\overline{x}_k}$ is the domain of variable x_k.

Example:

Assume $Z = \{z_1, z_2, z_3\}$. If we follow the same instantiation order in X, the search starts with the domain of z_1 which is $\{1\ 2\}$. The first branching produces two alternate partial labelings: $\{(1)(2)\}$ which are derived from d_{z_1}

At this stage $X_{k=1} = \{z_1\}$ and the set of future variables $F_{k=1} = \{z_2\ z_3\}$.

The next stage involves the instantiation of the second variable z_2 with domain $\{1\ 2\ 3\}$. These values are concatenated with the initial partial solutions shown above:

$$\{\ (1\ 1)\ (1\ 2)\ (1\ 3)\ (2\ 1)\ (2\ 2)\ (2\ 3)\ \} = d_{z_1} \times d_{z_2}$$

with $X_2 = \{z_1 z_2\}$ and $F_2 = \{z_3\}$. The third stage of the search gives:

$$d_{z_1} \times d_{z_2} \times d_{z_3} =$$

$$\{(1\ 1\ a)\ (1\ 2\ a)\ (1\ 3\ a)\ (2\ 1\ a)\ (2\ 2\ a)\ (2\ 3\ a)$$
$$(1\ 1\ b)\ (1\ 2\ b)\ (1\ 3\ b)\ (2\ 1\ b)\ (2\ 2\ b)\ (2\ 3\ b)\}$$

where $X_3 = \{z_1\ z_2\ z_3\}$ and $F_2 = \varnothing$

Forward Checking and Search

In the example above, we saw how search can be used to enumerate $\overline{Z}$.

It is possible to scan $\overline{Z}$ to find all the consistent labelings with respect to the constraints C and objectives O. This approach, however, is too inefficient. The forward checking algorithm propagates constraints during search. This is shown in the example below:

Example:

Consider, for a moment, the search tree at stage $k = 1$, where $X_k = \{z_1\}$ and the tree has only two partial labelings $\{(1)(2)\}$.

Consider the first labeling: $\overline{X}_k^1 = (1)$. Setting variable $z_1 = 1$ gives us a clue as to what values it's possible for z_2 to take. This is done by examining the constraints' CF value tables. Take for example the constraint c_1 which has $Z_1 = \{z_1, z_2\}$ and $T_1 = \{(22)(23)\}$. Clearly, setting z_1 to unity precludes z_2 from taking any of the values from its domain. This means that there is no consistent labeling with $z_1 = 1$. Consequently, the first labeling is dropped, effectively, eliminating half the search tree.

The idea of using a constraint to constrain the values of future variables in F_k based on values chosen for variables in X_k is called Forward Checking (it can also be viewed as a kind of Constraint Propagation).

At any stage of the search k, there is a set of instantiated variables X_k

and a set of future variables F_k. Forward checking is the process of filtering out inconsistent values from the domains of the future variables by checking the values of $x_i \in X_k$ against the constraints and objectives. In other words, the original domain d_f of some future variable $f \in F_k$ is subject to filtering at stage k. The filtering of future variables is done separately for each branch of the search tree. If $\overline{X}_k$ denotes a particular branch (partial labeling on X), then, the filtered domain of future variable f with respect to labeling $\overline{X}_k$ is denoted by $d_f^{\overline{X}_k}$, and is given by:

$$d_f^{\overline{X}_k} = \left\{ \overline{f} \mid \overline{f} \in d_f \ \wedge \ Z_j \langle \overline{X}_k \| \overline{f} \rangle \in T_j \ \forall_{j \in \Psi_{X_k \cup \{f\}}} \right\} \quad (A.4)$$

where $\overline{f}$ is a value from the domain of f and, where Ψ_A is defined as the set of all constraints that are applicable to the variables in set A. Where:

$$\Psi_A = \{ j \mid 1 \leq j < (c+h) \text{ and } Z_j \subseteq A \} \quad (A.5)$$

In the definition of $d_f^{\overline{X}_k}$, Ψ is taken over all constraints and objectives $(c+h)$.

$d_f^{\overline{X}_k}$, is defined as set of all values in d_f that pass the filtering test. This means that if f was to be the next variable for instantiation, then only the members of $d_f^{\overline{X}_k}$ will survive all the applicable constraints and objectives. When this filtering is applied to all f in F_k we get the filtered set of future domains:

$$\mathbf{d}^{\overline{X}_k} = \{ d_f^{\overline{X}_k} \mid \forall_{f \in F_k} \} \quad (A.6)$$

The Forward Checking Algorithm

The forward checking algorithm has two basic steps: instantiation and forward-checking of future variables.

The algorithm (FORW-CHECK) takes two arguments, a labeling and the current variable being instantiated. The algorithm starts with k = 0, $X_k = 0$ and $F_k = Z$:-

FORW-CHECK $(\overline{X}_k, k)$

   1. IF $k = n$

   THEN return $\{ \overline{X}_k \}$

   2. Compute $d^{\overline{X}_k}$
using equation ((A.6))

   3. IF $(k \le n$ and $\varnothing \in d^{\overline{X}_k})$
THEN   return $\varnothing$

   ELSE return $\left\{ \text{UNION of FORW-CHECK}(\overline{X}_k \| \overline{x}_{k+1} \quad k+1) \right\}$

(taken over all $\overline{x}_{k+1}$ in the filtered set $d^{\overline{X}}_{x_{k+1}}$)

The algorithm starts with the call FORW-CHECK($\{\varnothing\}$, 0). The algorithm returns all the consistent and optimal labelings in the state space of labelings. If it returns $\varnothing$, there are no feasible solutions among the successors of the node in question.

Example

Let S-TREE be a list that denotes the set of all partial and complete labelings being considered at any stage of the search.

<u>Stage 0</u> $k = 0$ and $n = 3$, $X_n = \{ \varnothing \} F_0 = Z$

S-TREE $= \{\varnothing\}$

$d^{\overline{X}_k} = \{(1\,2)(1\,2\,3)(a\,b)\}$

<u>Stage 1</u> $k = 1$, $n = 3$, $X_k = \{ z_1 \}$ $F_1 = \{ z_2\, z_3 \}$

S-TREE $= \{(1)\,(2)\}$

for $\underline{X_k = (1)}, d^{\overline{X}_k} = \{ \varnothing\,(a\,b) \}$

for $X_k = (2)$, $d^{\overline{X}k} = \{(2\ 3)\ (a\ b)\ \}$[35]

Stage 2 k = 2, n = 3, $X_k = \{z_1\ z_2\}F_2=\{\ z_3\ \}$

S-TREE $= \{(2\ 2)(2\ 3)\}$

for $X_k = (2\ 2)$, $d^{\overline{X}k} = \{(a)\}$

for $X_k = (2\ 3)$, $d^{\overline{X}k} = \{\varnothing\}$

Stage 3 k = 3, n = 3, $X_k = Z$ and $F_n = \{\varnothing\}$

The labeling (2 2 a) is returned as the only consistent labeling in the state space of labelings.

In addition to CLPs, we also have seen how a CLOP can be represented with binary constraints and objectives and can then be solved by forward checking. The problem with using this approach is that very few CLOPs have perfect solutions. Multi-objective problems often tend to be over-constrained, there are usually no solutions that satisfy all constraints and optimize all objectives simultaneously. CLOPs often have to be solved by relaxing the constraints and by making tradeoffs among the objectives.

SOLVING THE CLOP

Problems that have many constraints and many objectives are liable to be over constrained. The only way a solution can be found is through the relaxation of the constraints and objectives. By relaxing an objective, we imply the making of tradeoffs among objectives. Formally, an over-constrained situation is said to have occurred when at some stage of the search k (where k < n) we have:

$$\exists f[\ d_f^{\overline{X}k} = \{\varnothing\}]\quad \forall_{\overline{X}_k\ \in\ S\text{-}TREE}$$

Example

---

[35]We get the set (a b) because only arc consistency is maintained in this example, no path consistency is checked [Mackworth 77].

To illustrate the the notion of an over-constrained CLOP, let us now introduce yet another objective into the current example.

The second objective o_5 has CF_5:   Maximize: $2(z_1^2 - z_2)$

The values in the table are:

CF_4	z2 = 1	z2 = 2	z2 = 3
z1 = 1	2	0	-1
z1 = 2	7	6	5

Converting the values into ranks, we get the following table for CF_5:

CF_4	z2 = 1	z2 = 2	z2 = 3
z1 = 1	N	N	N
z1 = 2	1	N	N

Consequently, $Z_5 = \{z_1\, z_2\}$ and $T_5 = \{(2\,1)\}$

In the previous section we saw that there was only one consistent labeling (2 2 a). This solution is rendered inconsistent by objective o_5. Now, the only way to find a solution is by relaxation of the constraints or by trading off among objectives.

Overconstrained problems are solved by relaxing the constraints and objectives. In order to be able to do so, we need a way of representing the constraints and objectives which will allow relaxation. This is discussed below.

Representing Relaxable Constraints and Objectives

Hereafter, we will refer to both constraints and objectives as criteria. A criterion is denoted by ω_j and, the set of all criteria is Ω where $|\Omega| = (c + h)$, the total number of constraints and objectives. Each criterion ω_j has an associated function CF_j with a corresponding value matrix. As before, Z_j is the set of variables that ω_j acts on.

In the previous section we defined a consistent labeling on Z as one that obtained a CF value of 1 for all the criteria in Ω , we will relax this requirement now.

Definition. Let $S_{\underline{z}}$ be a set that represents the CF values obtained for all

the criterion by the labeling $\overline{Z}$.

$$S_{\overline{Z}} = \left\{ r_{\overline{Z},1}, \ r_{\overline{Z},2}, \ \cdots \ r_{\overline{Z},(c+h)} \right\} \qquad (A.7)$$

Where $r_{\overline{Z},j}$ is the *CF* value of the jth criterion for the labeling $\overline{Z}$. The value $r_{\overline{Z},j}$ is called the rank of the jth criterion and S is called the *spectrum* of $\overline{Z}$. A labeling is consistent and ideally optimal if it is complete over Z and has all ranks = 1.

Relaxing CF$_j$. Each criterion ω_j has a corresponding function CF_J.

The function call $CF_j(\overline{Z}_j)$ returns a value in the set J_1^N, where N is some arbitrarily large number. This value is called the rank of the jth criterion. Although $\overline{Z}_j$ which obtains ranks of 1 for all the criteria continues to be the best possible labeling, other $\overline{Z}_J$ values that obtain $r_{\overline{Z}_{j'},j}$ greater than 1 are considered to be incompatible with the original ω_j but compatible with relaxations of the criterion ω_j.

Optimality as non-dominance. We need some way of differentiating among the spectra of different $\overline{X}_k$ at some level k. If there are some spectra with all ranks = 1, then clearly, these partial solutions are the best possible and should be selected for future instantiation. However, we may have a situation in which all the spectra are suboptimal. Therefore, we need a measure of suboptimality. For example, if we had three spectra $S^1 = \{2\ 3\ 2\}$, $S^2 = \{3\ 6\ 5\}$ $S^3 = \{1\ 5\ 3\}$, then S^1 dominates S^2 with respect to all the criteria because it has better ranks in its spectrum.

Representing the search tree. At any stage k there may be several labelings of X_k. The set of all labelings at any level of the search is stored in a search tree denoted by S-TREE$_k$. The pth labeling in this set is denoted by $\overline{X}_k^p$. Any particular labeling $\overline{X}_k^p$ is said to be non-dominated if there is no other labeling that has all ranks in its spectrum better than the ranks in $S_{\overline{X}_k^p}$.

Determining the Ranks for partial labelings

A particular rank $r_{\underset{z,j}{}}$ is given by the function call to CF_j with the

argument $\overline{Z}_j \langle \overline{Z} \rangle$. The question is: How does one evaluate the rank of a partial labeling that has insufficient data for a given CF_j ? If, for example, $\exists z_i \; [z_i \in Z_j \;\; \wedge \;\; z_i \notin X_k]$ then it is not possible to

get $\overline{Z}_j \langle \overline{X}_k \rangle$. For example, if $Z_j = \{z_1 \, z_3 \, z_5\}$ and $X_k = \{z_1 \, z_2 \, z_3\}$ with $F_k = \{z_4 \, z_5 \, z_6\}$, then evaluating CF_j requires that we know the value of z_5 which is actually a future variable.

We can, at best, make an estimate of the unknown ranks. One approach is to find the ranks of all possible completions of the partial labeling and choose the minimum. This can be done without actually searching the space of labelings but by searching the CF table for a minimum value. For example, if variable $f \in Z_j$ and $f \notin X_k$, then its rank can be estimated as:

$$r_{\underset{X_k,j}{}} = MIN \left[\; CF_j(\overline{Z}_j \; \langle \overline{X}_k \| \overline{f}_1 \rangle), CF_j(\overline{Z}_j \; \langle \overline{X}_k \| \overline{f}_2 \rangle), \; \cdots \right.$$

$$\left. CF_j(\overline{Z}_j \; \langle \overline{X}_k \| \overline{f}_3 \rangle) \right] \tag{A.8}$$

where $d_f^{X_k} = \{\overline{f}_1 \overline{f}_2 \overline{f}_3 \; \cdots \; \overline{f}_i\}$

Note that the filtered (forward checked) domain is used for the future variable f. Further, the above equation assumes that X_k is short of Z_j by only one future variable. This form, however, will work even if there are many future variables, in which case, the terms in the equation above will be replaced by the elements of the power set of the domains of the future variables. This is shown in the example below:

The equation above represents a heuristic for evaluating the branches of the search. We will later prove that this heuristic is *admissible* [Hart, Nilsson & Raphael 68], and that the algorithms based on such heuristics guarantee that solutions will be non-dominated over the entire search space.

AN ADMISSIBLE ALGORITHM FOR A CLOP

In this section we will examine CLOPS, an algorithm for solving Consistent Labeling Optimization Problems.

The CLOPS algorithm:

1. Put the start node in *S–TREE*, and set the list *ANSWERS* = $\emptyset$.

2. IF *S–TREE* = $\emptyset$ THEN exit with *ANSWERS*, ELSE continue

3. Calculate the spectrum for each labeling in *S–TREE* using Equation ((A.8)) to calculate those ranks which need to be estimated

4. Select all non-dominated labelings in *S–TREE* by comparing *S–TREE* over the set { *S–TREE* ‖ *ANSWERS* }. Put the selected labelings in in a list called *ND*. Put the rest in another list ¬ *ND*

5. Select all the complete labelings in *ND* and transfer them to the list *ANSWERS*.
   IF any answers are found and IF others are not needed, THEN STOP
      ELSE, IF more solutions are needed, THEN continue on to the next step.

6. IF *ND* = $\emptyset$, THEN return *ANSWERS* and STOP, ELSE continue

7. Expand the labelings in *ND* to give ND_{new}

8. Set $S–TREE$ = { ND_{new} ‖ ¬ *ND* }

9. GOTO step 2

At this point, we will go back to our continuing example to illustrate how the CLOPS algorithm is applied, and why the estimating heuristic used above is guaranteed to lead to optimal solutions. Readers who feel the example is unnecessary may safely skip it.

Example:

We have a total of five criteria (three constraints and two objectives). The first step: converting the criteria into a relaxable form.

For example: CF_1 is : $(2z_1)^2 + z_2^2 \geq 18$

The values obtained for different combinations of z_1 and z_2 are:

actual	z2 = 1	z2 = 2	z2 = 3
z1 = 1	5	8	13
z1 = 2	17	20	25

This matrix can be ranked as shown below:

CF_1	z2 = 1	z2 = 2	z2 = 3
z1 = 1	N	N	N
z1 = 2	2	1	1

Where the labeling ($z_1 = 2$, $z_2 = 1$) is given a rank of 2 because the value 17 is close to the best. The determination of the rank is a different problem. There are several informal ways of determining the rank of sub-optimal labelings, but here we will assume that ranks are input at the discretion of the user. Using this technique, all the other CF matrices are changed as shown below:

Ranks for CF_2:

CF_2	z2 = 1	z2 = 2	z2 = 3
z1 = 1	N	2	1
z1 = 2	2	1	1

Ranks for CF_3 (chosen arbitrarily):

CF_3	z2 = 1	z2 = 2	z2 = 3
z3 = a	N	3	N
z3 = b	1	1	N

Ranks for CF_4:

CF_4	z2 = 1	z2 = 2	z2 = 3
z1 = 1	N	N	N
z1 = 2	1	1	1

Ranks for CF_5:

CF_5	z2 = 1	z2 = 2	z2 = 3
z1 = 1	N	N	N
z1 = 2	1	2	3

the spectrum of any labeling will have the ranks from CF_1 to CF_5

Let us work through the staged search process

Stage 0: $k = 0$, $n = 3$

$X_k = \{\emptyset\}$ $F_k = \{z_1 z_2 z_3\}$

$S\text{-}TREE = \{\emptyset\}$

Stage 1: $k = 1$, $n = 3$

$X_k = \{z_1\}$

$S\text{-}TREE = \{(1)(2)\} = \{\overline{X}^1_k \ \overline{X}^2_k\}$

The first step is to forward check with respect to each $\overline{X}_k$ in $S\text{-}TREE$.

$\overline{X}^1_k$ and CF_1 lead to a $\{\emptyset\}$ for the future variable z_2, hence $\overline{X}^1_k$ is

eliminated. Turning to $\overline{X}^2_k$, we get no changes through forward checking, consequently:

$S\text{-}TREE = \{(2)\}$

The next step is to find the spectrum, which is: $S_{\overline{X}^2_k} = \{11111\}$

The spectrum is calculated for each CF by looking for the lowest rank possible given the condition that z_1 is already set to 2.

Stage 2: $k = 2$, $n = 3$

$X_k = \{z_1 z_2\}$

$S\text{-}TREE = \{(21)(22)(23)\} = \{\overline{X}^1_k \ \overline{X}^2_k \ \overline{X}^3_k\}$

$d^{\overline{X}^1_k}_{z_3} = \{b\}$, $S_{\overline{X}^1_k} = \{22111\}$

$d^{\overline{X}^2_k}_{z_3} = \{ab\}$, $S_{\overline{X}^2_k} = \{11112\}$

$d^{\overline{X}^3_k}_{z_3} = \{\emptyset\}$, $S_{\overline{X}^3_k} = \{no \quad use \quad calculating \quad this\}$

Since $\overline{X}^1{}_k$ and $\overline{X}^2{}_k$ are both non-dominated, any one of the two may be chosen for further expansion. Let's assume $\overline{X}^2{}_k$ is chosen:

Stage 3: k = 3, n = 3

$S\text{-}TREE = \{(21)(22a)(22b)\} = \{\overline{X}^1_k \ \overline{X}^2_k \ \overline{X}^3_k\}$

The corresponding spectra are: $\{(22111)(11312)(11112)\}$.

Consequently, $\overline{X}^3_k$ emerges as the first complete non-dominated solution. **This solution is guaranteed to be non-dominated over the entire state space,** even though the space has only been partially enumerated. A rigorous proof of this condition is provided in the next section.

Proof of Optimality of the CLOPS algorithm

Lemma1 In a partial labeling $\overline{X}_k$ estimated rank of a criterion ω_i: $r_{\underline{X_{k,j}}}$ is liable to remain constant or increase in further instantiations of the partial labeling $\overline{X}_k$. If and only if $r_{\underline{X_{k,j}}}$ is estimated using equation ((A.8)).

Proof Consider a partial labeling over the variables X_k. To calculate the rank of criterion ω_j for labelings $\overline{X}_k$ when $\exists f[f \in Z_j \ \wedge \ f \notin X_k]$ then, an estimate is needed. Any arbitrary expansion of $\overline{X}_k$ is given by:

$$\overline{X}_{k+1} = (\overline{X}_k \| \overline{f}) \text{ where } \overline{f} \in d_f^{\overline{X}_k}$$

The set of all such labelings (children of $\overline{X}_k$) is denoted by $\{\overline{X}_{k+1}\} \subseteq S\text{-}TREE_{k+1}$. In **Lemma1** we assumed that the ranks will be calculated using equation (A.8). This means that $r_{\underline{X_k}}$ is the minimum of the ranks in all $\overline{X}^i_{k+1} \in \{\overline{X}_{k+1}\}$. Consequently,

$$\forall_{\overline{X}^i_{k+1} \in \{\overline{X}_{k+1}\}} \left[r_{\underline{X_{k,j}}} \leq r_{\underline{X_{k+1,j}}} \right]$$

where, $\overline{X}^i_{k+1}$ is a child of node of $\overline{X}^j_k$, and where i and j are valid integers.

QED

Corollary to Lemma1: An estimated rank $r_{\overline{x}_k,j}$, once estimated using (A.8), can never decrease in value.

Proof As the estimated ranks are the minimum possible for all combinations of future variables, the rank's value cannot decrease in when future variables are expanded.

Theorem1 A partial labeling $\overline{X}_k$ that is non-dominated in the set S–TREE will remain non-dominated as long as it is not instantiated further. This holds regardless of the number of instantiations carried out

on the other $\overline{X}$ in the S–TREE.

Proof Let there be a partial labeling $\overline{X}^1_k \in$ S–TREE . Let $\overline{X}^1_k$ be among the non-dominated labelings.

Let us assume that $\overline{X}^1_k$ is kept unchanged while instantiations are made on other non-dominated labelings.

If $\overline{X}^1_k$ is to be dominated by some future instantiation:

$\overline{X}^i_{k+\delta} \in$ S–TREE , where $i \neq 1$ and δ is some arbitrary number of instantiations, such that $k + \delta \leq$ the total number of possible

instantiations, then the ranks in the spectrum of $\overline{X}^i_k$ have to decrease in value. This violates the Corollary to **_Lemma1_** and hence, by

contradiction, $\overline{X}^1_k$ cannot be dominated by $\overline{X}^i_{k+\delta} \in$ S–TREE .

QED

We will now prove the optimality of the CLOPS algorithm. The proof is based on that suggested for the A^* algorithm [Hart, Nilsson & Raphael 68, Pearl 84]

Let's start with some useful definitions:

Definition. Let B denote the beginning root node and let Γ denote the set of non-dominated complete labelings on Z.

Definition. Let S–TREE denote the set of all labelings (partial or complete) in the search tree.

Definition. Let *ND* denote the set of non-dominated labelings in *S–TREE*.

Definition. Let *ND*(T) denote a function that extracts the non-dominated labeling from a set of labelings T .

Definition. Let ↑, ~ and ↓ be indicators of dominance, non-dominance and inferiority respectively. These three relations are defined below:

If there is a labeling α and a set of mutually non-dominated labelings β, then:

IF $PO(\alpha\|\beta) = (\alpha\|\beta)$ THEN, α is said to be non dominating over β. This is denoted as $\alpha \sim \{\beta\}$.

IF $PO(\alpha\|\beta) = \beta$ THEN, α is said to be inferior over β. This is denoted as $\alpha \downarrow \{\beta\}$.

IF $PO(\alpha\|\beta) = \alpha$ THEN, $\alpha \uparrow \{\beta\}$.

Theorem2. The first complete solution that the CLOPS algorithm will terminate with is guaranteed to be non-dominated over the entire state space of *Z*.

Proof Suppose CLOPS terminates with a solution *l* such that $l \downarrow \{\Gamma\}$.

From the definition of CLOPS we know that the algorithm terminates whenever a node it selects for expansion turns out to be complete. The algorithm only selects those nodes which are non-dominated over the entire *S–TREE*. Consequently, $l \sim \{S–TREE\}$. But as we assumed that $l \downarrow \{\Gamma\}$, it follows that $S–TREE \downarrow \{\Gamma\}$.

In other words, $\forall_{\overline{X} \in S-TREE} \quad [\overline{X} \downarrow \Gamma]$.

However, as Γ is in the state space, it has to be derived by instantiating nodes in *S–TREE*, and as $S–TREE \downarrow \{\Gamma\}$, it follows that:

$\exists \overline{X}_k \in S-TREE$ such that one of its descendants $\overline{X}_n$
is a member of Γ,where, $n \geq k$

It then follows that: $\overline{X}_n \uparrow \overline{X}_k$ where, $n \geq k$

This violates ***Theorem1*** which states that none of the instantiations of a node can dominate the node. Hence, by contradiction, CLOPS will terminate with a solution that is non-dominated over Γ.

Q.E.D.

CONCLUSIONS

The CLOPS algorithm is applicable to a large number of engineering problems that involve a mix of constraints and objectives that may be non-linear, non-monotonic and even non-continuous. The algorithm is a modified form of the A^* algorithm. CLOPS is different in that, it is applicable to multi-objective problems and uses non-dominance as a measure of optimality. The CLOPS algorithm is based on ideas drawn from both the A^* literature of Artificial Intelligence and the Multi-Criteria decision making literature of Operations Research.

Appendix B
A Trace of CYCLOPS in Action

In order to understand the workings of the CYCLOPS program we must start by showing how data, knowledge, and decisions are input into the system.

CYCLOPS ARCHITECTURE

The CYCLOPS architecture is shown in Figure B-1.

As we have noted, the **user** watches designs as they are being detailed and developed and can guide the program through the design process, by doing several things:

- accepting or discarding a design, or

- invoking the adaptation process, or

- invoking the exploration module, or just

- letting the normal search process continue.

The normal search process involves branching and selection. These two steps are carried out by the **synthesizer** and the **selector**. The synthesizer takes partial designs and adds detail to them by instantiating their variables. The selector performs two functions. The selector first hands off the design to a precedent manager. This is done to check for any new problems or opportunities in the partial design. Next, the selector performs a pareto optimality check. It decides to place a design either in the active list or the dormant list.

The user can also invoke the **explorer**. This module simply relaxes criteria and hands off, to the synthesizer, any new partial designs surfaced as a result of the relaxation. The rest of the process is the same as that of the normal search process.

Finally, the user may decide to adapt a particular design. When the design adapter is invoked, it searches the partial design for problems

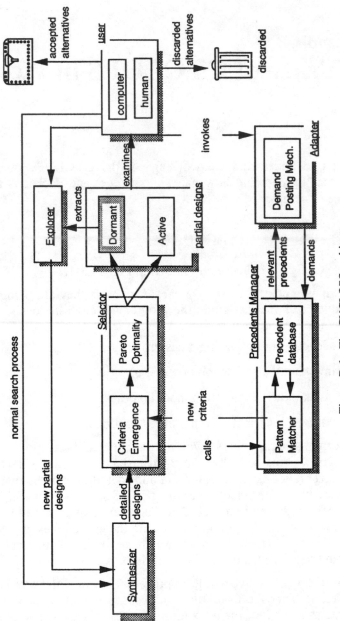

Figure B-1: The CYCLOPS architecture

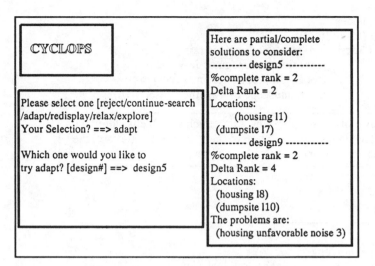

Figure B-2: The CYCLOPS interface

and uses the *demand posting* mechanism to post demands on the **precedents manager**. If a relevant precedent is found, it is retrieved and applied to the design problem by the **adapter**.

The interface to CYCLOPS is shown in Figure B-2. The interface has two windows, a prompting and command input window (left) and a window for viewing alternatives (on the right).

AN EXAMPLE

In this section we will see how a design problem is posed and how precedents are represented. The example used here is a modified version of the problem introduced in Chapter 2.

The problem statement.
The design involves the siting of a sector of housing, an apartment complex, a dumpsite, a recreational area and a cemetery. The program CYCLOPS needs this data to be input as LISP lists. All commentary provided in the trace are boxed.

The atom *nodes* represents the root node.
Data about the landscape is stored at the root. This information is inherited by all the branches.

```
(set '*nodes*
   '((( (name (root))
      (description ((root landscape is rainy)
                  (root sound propagates-in-waves)
                  (root light propagates-in-waves)
                  (root landscape in washington-state))))))
```

> The variables are stored in a list. Each variable is stored with
> its domain and a description of the variable. In this case, the
> variables are landuses that have to be sited.

```
(set '*variables*
   '(
;-------------------------------------------

((name (housing-sector-1))
 (domain ( lot7 lot10 lot12  lot9 lot11 ))
 (description ( (housing-sector-1 is-a landuse)
          (housing-sector-1 is-a low-rise-building)
          (housing-sector-1 is-a building) )))


((name (apartment-complex))
 (domain ( lot7 lot10 lot12  lot9 lot11 ))
 (description ( (apartment-complex is-a landuse)
          (apartment-complex is-a high-rise-building)
          (apartment-complex is-a building) )))

((name (dumpsite))
 (domain (lot3 lot5 ))
 (description ()))

((name (recreational-area))
 (domain ( lot7 lot10 lot12  lot9 lot11 ))
 (description ()))


((name (cemetery))
 (domain (lot3 lot5 ))
 (description ()))


;-------------------------------------------
))
```

> Each of the values of the variable's domains are also described.
> The lots of land have to be described. The descriptions are stored
> in the form of a list, and provides an X-Y location
> and properties local to the site.

```
(set '*values*
'(
;------------------------------------------

( (name (lot3))
  (description ((location 250 550)
          (lot3 next-to sewage-treatment-plant))))

( (name (lot5))
  (description ((location 250 400)
          (lot5 next-to sewage-treatment-plant))))

( (name (lot4))
  (description ((location 350 400))))

( (name (lot8))
  (description ((location 350 300))))

( (name (lot7))
  (description ((location 450 450)
          (next-to highway))))

( (name (lot9))
  (description ((slope rank 2)
          (location 450 300)
          (ground has slope))))

( (name (lot11))
  (description ( (slope rank 6)
          (can-view lake)
          (can-view power-lines)
          (location 500 300)
          (ground has slope)) ))

( (name (lot17))
  (description ( (slope rank 6)
          (can-view lake)
          (can-view power-lines)
          (location 600 250)
          (ground has slope))) )
```

```
( (name (lot14))
  (description ( (location 450 200))))

( (name (lot16))
  (description ( (location 550 150)) ))

( (name (lot15))
  (description ( (location 450 100))))

( (name (lot10))
  (description ( (location 500 400)
        (lot10 next-to lake)
        (soil rank 6)) ))

( (name (lot12))
  (description ( (location 550 400)
        (lot12 next-to lake)
        (soil rank 6))))


;-------------------------------------------
))
```

> The Δ_g is denoted in the system as *delta*.
> The starting value of *delta* is 0 (zero[th] order design)

```
(set '*delta* 0)  ; starting delta value
```

> To help CYCLOPS reason across precedents, a domain
> specific dictionary is to be provided. Currently, CYCLOPS'
> method of handling similar words is crude, as the following
> code shows.

```
; the object hierarchy

;dwellings
(putprop 'dwelling 'buildings 'is-a)
(putprop 'house 'dwelling 'is-a)
(putprop 'housing 'dwelling 'is-a)
(putprop 'home 'dwelling 'is-a)
(putprop 'housing-sector-1 'dwelling 'is-a)
(putprop 'housing-sector-2 'dwelling 'is-a)
(putprop 'apartment-complex 'dwelling 'is-a)

;commercial
```

```
(putprop 'commercial 'buildings 'is-a)
(putprop 'shop 'commercial 'is-a)
(putprop 'office 'commercial 'is-a)
(putprop 'hospital 'commercial 'is-a)
(putprop 'hotel 'commercial 'is-a)

;educational
(putprop 'educational 'buildings 'is-a)
(putprop 'school 'educational 'is-a)
(putprop 'schooling 'educational 'is-a)
(putprop 'college 'educational 'is-a)

;land
(putprop 'planar-object 'inanimate-thing 'is-a)
(putprop 'land 'planar-object 'is-a)
(putprop 'landscape 'land 'is-a)
(putprop 'site 'land 'is-a)
(putprop 'ground 'land 'is-a)

;misc
(putprop 'buildings 'rectangular-prism 'is-a)
(putprop 'rectangular-prism 'inanimate-thing 'is-a)
(putprop 'inanimate-thing 'thing)

;end of object hierarchy
;-----------------------------------------------
```

Domain Knowledge-Base: The Precedents

The list of precedents used by CYCLOPS is very short and should be several thousand times larger in order to show true intelligent behavior. Currently CYCLOPS has a flat, one-level indexing mechanism which is slow.

Precedents are defined by the **defprecedent** function. These precedents are compiled into rules, as shown for the first precedent listed below. The rules are derived directly from the precedent. The rules are then fed into a production system[36].

```
; The PRECEDENTS
;


;**********************************************************************
; A precedent about how people in thailand keep their homes form
; flooding


(defprecedent thailand-stilts
 (conditions1
  (and (on hut ground)
     (is ground flooded)))

 (effects1 (unfavorable house-is-flooded (rank 8)))

 (explanations1
  (because (unfavorable house-is-flooded (rank 8))
       (is building flooded))

  (because (is building flooded)
       (and (on building ground)
          (is ground flooded))))

 (action (on building stilts))

 (effects2 (not (unfavorable house-is-flooded (rank 8))))

 (explanations2
  (because (not (unfavorable house-is-flooded (rank 8)))
       (and (not (on ground flooded))
```

---

[36]The production system used is **IMST** [Navinchandra 85]. The rules are represented as lists. A rule has a IF part and a THEN part separated by an arrow. Propositions are added and removed from the working memory with the **assert** and **unassert** commands. Variables in IMST are denoted by angle brackets. For example: <variable1>

```
              (is ground flooded)))

       (because (not (on building ground))
              (<action>))))

; the translation into rules

;(rule thailand-stilts-1
;      (on hut ground)
;      (is ground flooded)
; -->  (is hut flooded)
;      (assert because
;            (is hut flooded)
;            ((is ground flooded)
;             (on hut ground))))
;
;(rule thailand-stilts-2
;      (is hut flooded)
; -->  (assert unfavorable house-is-flooded (rank 8))
;      (assert because
;            (unfavorable house-is-flooded (rank <rank>))
;            ((is hut flooded))))
;
;(rule thailand-stilts-3
;      (is-a hut landuse)
;      (wanted (not (unfavorable house-is-flooded (rank <anyrank>))))
; -->  (assert action (on hut stilts))
;      (unassert (wanted
;            (not (unfavorable house-is-flooded (rank <anyrank>]
;
;(rule thailand-stilts-4
;      (wanted (not (on hut ground)))
;      (on hut ground)
; -->  (assert action (on hut stilts))
;      (unassert wanted (not (on hut ground)))
;      (unassert on hut ground)
;      (assert because
;            (not (on hut ground))
;            ((on hut ground) (action (on hut stilts)))))

;********************************************************************
; light transports itself from one point to another as long
; as there are no obstructions

(defprecedent transport-light
  (conditions
   (and (at person place1)
        (next-to place1 place2)
        (not (between place1 place2 anything))))

  (effects (unobstructed-path-between place1 place2))
```

```
(explanations
 (because (unobstructed-path-between place1 place2)
        (and (at person place1)
             (next-to place1 place2)
             (not (between place1 place2 anything))))))
```

```
;********************************************************************
; A precedent about how ugly highways can be.

(defprecedent ugly-sight
 (acquired "Many years ago, at my aunt's place")

 (conditions (and (at building site)
                  (next-to site  highway)
                  (not (between highway site anything))))

 (effects (unfavorable ugly-highway (rank 5))
          (say Oh No The <building> is too close to the ugly highway))

 (explanations
  (because (unfavorable ugly-highway (rank 5))
          (unobstructed-path-between building highway))

  (because (unobstructed-path-between building highway)
          (and (precedent transport-light)
               (at building site)
               (next-to site highway)
               (not (between highway site anything))))))
```

```
;********************************************************************
; A precedent about how noisy a highway can be

; highway noise precedent

(defprecedent ugly-highway-noise
 (acquired "Many years ago, at my aunt's place")

 (conditions (at building site)
             (next-to site highway)
             (not (between highway site anything)))

 (effects (unfavorable highway-noise (rank 5))
          (say Oh No The <house> is too close to the noisy highway))

 (explanations
  (because (unfavorable highway-noise (rank 5))
          (and (unobstructed-path-between site highway))))


  (because (unobstructed-path-between site highway)
```

```
        (and (precedent transport-light)
            (at building  site)
            (next-to site highway)
            (not (between highway site anything))))))
```

```
;*********************************************************************
; The power lines are ugly to look at
```

```
(defprecedent power-lines-ugly
  (conditions (and (at building site)
              (can-view site power-lines)))
```

```
  (effect (unfavorable power-lines-in-view (rank 4)))
```

```
  (because (unfavorable power-lines-in-view (rank 4))
        (and (at building site)
            (can-view site power-lines))))
```

```
;*********************************************************************
; an object on a sloped surface is tilted
```

```
(defprecedent sloped-object
  (conditions (and (on object ground)
              (is ground tilted )))
  (effects (is object tilted))
```

```
  (explanations
    (because (is object tilted)
          (and (on object ground)
              (is ground tilted)))))
```

```
;*********************************************************************
; A precedent about homes on steep hillsides
```

```
(defprecedent slope-rank
  (acquired "nepal, while trekking")
```

```
  (conditions (building is tilted)
        (slope <rank> >= 3))
```

```
  (effects (unfavorable slope (rank <rank>))
        (say The slope at the  site is too high.))
```

```
  (explanations
    (because (unfavorable slope (rank <rank>))
          (building is tilted)
          (slope <rank> >= 3)
```

```
              (precedent sloped-object))))


;*******************************************************
; dumpsites are bad places. Being within 200 m of one is
; really bad!

(defprecedent avoid-dumpsites
  (conditions (distance-between building  dumpsite) <= 200m)

  (effects (unfavorable dumpsite-close-by (rank 6)))

  (explanations
   (because (unfavorable dumpsite-close-by (rank 6))
        (distance-between building dumpsite) <= 200m)))



;*******************************************************
;sewage plants are like Ugh!
;


(defprecedent sewage-plants-are-bad
  (conditions (and (at building site)
            (next-to site sewage-treatment-plant)))

  (effects (unfavorable close-to-sewage-plant (rank 9))
        (say Ugh! I notice that the <building> is near a sewage plant.))

  (explanations
   (because   (unfavorable close-to-sewage-plant (rank 9))
        (and (building at site)
            (site next-to sewage-treatment-plant)))))


;*********************************************************************
; Avoid bad soil. A precedent picked up in a geo-technical class

(defprecedent bad-soil
  (conditions (and (building at site)
            (site soil <rank>  >= 3)))

  (effects (unfavorable soil-conditions (rank <rank>))
        (say Bad soil conditions for the <context has been detected.)))

  (explanations
   (because (unfavorable soil-conditions (rank <rank>))
        (and (building at site)
            (site soil <rank> >= 3)))))
```

```
;************************************************
; A precedent about my parent's home that was next to a lake
;

(defprecedent childhood-home-next-to-lake
 (conditions
  (and (at home site)
     (next-to site lake)))

 (effects (favorable home-next-to-lake (rank -3)
       (say The home being next to a lake reminds
          me of my parent's home.)))

 (explanation
  (because (favorable home-next-to-lake (rank -3))
        (and (at home site)
           (next-to site lake)))))


;************************************************
; a precedent about how an army  uses camouflage in battle

(defprecedent camouflage-used-in-war
 (conditions1 (can-view person barracks))

 (effects1 (unfavorable barracks-can-be-seen (rank 10)))

 (explanations1 (because (<effects1>) (<conditions1>)))

 (action (camouflage the barracks with green paint and plant-matter))

 (effects2 (not (unfavorable barracks-can-be-seen (rank 10))))

 (explanations2
  (because (not (unfavorable barracks-can-be-seen (rank 10)))
        (not (can-view person barracks)))

  (because (not (can-view person barracks))
        (<action>))))


;************************************************
;no two things can be at the same place at the same time

(defprecedent no-overlap
 (conditions (object1 at place1)
        (object2 at place1))

 (effect (unfavorable CONFLICT-overlap (rank 1000)))

 (explanations
  (because (unfavorable CONFLICT-overlap (rank 1000))
```

```
      (and (object1 at place1)
           (object2 at place1)))))

;*********************************************************************
; this is a simple constraint that is retrieved from memory
; and posed to the problem


(defprecedent recreational-area-should-be-next-to-lake
  (conditions
      (and (at recreational-area site)
         (not (next-to site  lake))))

  (effects ( unfavorable because-no-lake-nearby (rank 5)))

  (explanations
   (because ( unfavorable because-no-lake-nearby (rank 5))
          (and (at recreational-area  site)
             (not (next-to site lake))))))

;*********************************************************************
; the cemetery should not be visible

(defprecedent cemetery-should-not-be-seen-easily
  (conditions
   (and (at cemetery site1)
      (at building site2)
      (is building high-rise-building)
      ((distance-between site1 site2) <= 300m)))

  (effects (unfavorable cemetery-visible (rank 7)
         (say I think the cemetery is visible
           to the high-rising <building>))))

  (explanations
   (because (unfavorable cemetery-visible (rank 7))
          (and (cemetery at site1)
             (building at site2)
             (building is high-rise-building)
             ((distance-between site1 site2) <= 300m)))))


;*********************************************************************
; it is nice to have a lake visible from the dwellings

(defprecedent lake-visible-from-dwellings-is-nice
  (conditions
   (and (housing at site)
      (can-view site  lake)))

  (effects (favorable lake-visible (rank -5)
         (say That is nice the <housing> can  view  the lake))))
```

```
(explanations
 (because (favorable lake-visible (rank -5))
       (and (housing at site)
          (can-view site lake)))))



;*********************************************************************
; A precedent about a noise protection strategy

(defprecedent noise-protection-in-washington-state
 (acquired "While driving from Sea-tac to Tacoma")

 (conditions1
  (and (building at site1)
     (site1 next-to highway)
     (unobstructed-path-between site1 highway)))

 (effects1 (unfavorable highway-noise (rank 5)))

 (explanation1
  (because (unfavorable highway-noise (rank 5))
       (and (precedent ugly-highway-noise)
          (building at site1)
          (site1 next-to highway)
          (unobstructed-path-between site1 highway))))

 (action (plant a wall of trees between building and highway))

 (effects2 (not (unfavorable highway-noise (rank 5))))

 (explanation2
  (because (not (unfavorable highway-noise (rank 5)))
       (not (unobstructed-path-between site1 highway)))

  (because (not (unobstructed-path-between site1 highway))
       (and ( <action> )
          ( <explanation1>)))))
```

THE RUN

Here is a run the the CYCLOPS program. The run is annotated by boxed text and user input is in underlined bold **text**. The rest of the text is as it appeared in actual run, however, large parts of the trace has been edited out for brevity.

\<hera-16\> lisp

WELCOME TO CYCLOPS

Do you want audio prompt(ding-dong) ? [y/n] > **n**

Which data base? > **example**

Franz Lisp, Opus 42.16.3
(C) Copyright 1985, Franz Inc., Alameda Ca.

=> **(search-loop)**
The best delta value is: 10
This is value is liable to reduce/increase as we go along

> The program first shows the user the root node.
> This is only by convention.

Here are partial/complete solutions to consider:

--------------------- root ---------------------
%-complete rank = 10   Delta rank = 10
The locations of the landuses for root are:

Please select one:
[reject/automatic/continue-search/adapt/redisplay/relax/sort/quit/explore]

Your Selection? ==> **automatic**

> The user selects automatic mode. A controlling program takes
> the place of the user for a specified number of synthesis steps

How many steps automatic? > **5**
Starting search ...

Looking for Problems ....

Working on: design0

Working on: design1

Starting search ...
Looking for Problems ....

Working on: design2
Oh No The housing-sector-1 is too close to the ugly highway

Working on: design3
The housing-sector-1 being next to a lake reminds me of my parent 's home.
Bad soil conditions for the housing-sector-1 has been detected.

Working on: design6
That is nice the housing-sector-1 can has a view of the lake
The slope at the housing-sector-1 site is too high.

Working on: design7
Oh No The housing-sector-1 is too close to the ugly highway

Working on: design10

Looking for Problems ....

Working on: design12
Oh No The apartment-complex is too close to the ugly highway

> Notice how the program repeatedly discovers the same problem
> in different designs. This problem was discussed in Chapter 9

Working on: design13

Working on: design21
That is nice the apartment-complex can has a view of the lake
The slope at the apartment-complex site is too high.

Working on: design42
I think the cemetery is visible to the high-rising apartment-complex
The apartment-complex being next to a lake reminds me of my parent 's home.
Bad soil conditions for the apartment-complex has been detected.

> and so on........

> Finally, the program finds a complete solution. The
> Current *delta* value is 1

Here are some COMPLETE solutions to ponder...

--------------------- design48 ---------------------
%-complete rank = 0   Delta rank = 1
The locations of the landuses for design48 are:
(cemetery lot3)
(recreational-area lot10)
(apartment-complex lot12)
(housing-sector-1 lot9)
(dumpsite lot5)
The problems for design48 are
(apartment-complex unfavorable soil-conditions 6)
the opportunities of design48 are
(apartment-complex favorable home-next-to-lake -3)

Please Choose any of [reject-accept/redisplay/ignore]
Your response ==> **reject-accept**

> the user decides to accept the design

Give me a list of nodes you wish to accept ==> **(design48)**

> The user is not satisfied with the design and wants to explore,
> even though he has found a decent design.

Are you satisfied with what you have [y/n] ==> **n**

Please select one:
[reject/automatic/continue-search/adapt/redisplay/relax/sort/quit/explore]

Your Selection? ==> **relax**

> The user decides to call for a relaxation, pushing down
> the pareto surface

By how much [#] ==> **5**

Here are partial/complete solutions to consider:

--------------------- design16 ---------------------
%-complete rank = 3   Delta rank = 5
The locations of the landuses for design16 are:
(apartment-complex lot11)
(housing-sector-1 lot9)
(dumpsite lot3)
The problems for design16 are
(apartment-complex unfavorable slope 6)
(apartment-complex unfavorable power-lines-in-view 4)

the opportunities of design16 are
(apartment-complex favorable lake-visible -5)

--------------------- design21 ---------------------
%-complete rank = 3   Delta rank = 5
The locations of the landuses for design21 are:
(apartment-complex lot11)
(housing-sector-1 lot9)
(dumpsite lot5)
The problems for design21 are
(apartment-complex unfavorable slope 6)
(apartment-complex unfavorable power-lines-in-view 4)
the opportunities of design21 are
(apartment-complex favorable lake-visible -5)

--------------------- design22 ---------------------
%-complete rank = 1   Delta rank = 6
The locations of the landuses for design22 are:
(recreational-area lot7)
(apartment-complex lot10)
(housing-sector-1 lot9)
(dumpsite lot3)
The problems for design22 are
(recreational-area unfavorable because-no-lake-nearby 5)
(apartment-complex unfavorable soil-conditions 6)
the opportunities of design22 are
(apartment-complex favorable home-next-to-lake -3)

--------------------- design26 ---------------------
%-complete rank = 1   Delta rank = 6
The locations of the landuses for design26 are:
(recreational-area lot11)
(apartment-complex lot10)
(housing-sector-1 lot9)
(dumpsite lot3)
The problems for design26 are
(recreational-area unfavorable because-no-lake-nearby 5)
(apartment-complex unfavorable soil-conditions 6)
the opportunities of design26 are
(apartment-complex favorable home-next-to-lake -3)

--------------------- design27 ---------------------
%-complete rank = 1   Delta rank = 6
The locations of the landuses for design27 are:
(recreational-area lot7)
(apartment-complex lot12)
(housing-sector-1 lot9)
(dumpsite lot3)
The problems for design27 are
(recreational-area unfavorable because-no-lake-nearby 5)
(apartment-complex unfavorable soil-conditions 6)
the opportunities of design27 are

(apartment-complex favorable home-next-to-lake -3)

--------------------- design31 ---------------------
%-complete rank = 1   Delta rank = 6
The locations of the landuses for design31 are:
(recreational-area lot11)
(apartment-complex lot12)
(housing-sector-1 lot9)
(dumpsite lot3)
The problems for design31 are
(recreational-area unfavorable because-no-lake-nearby 5)
(apartment-complex unfavorable soil-conditions 6)
the opportunities of design31 are
(apartment-complex favorable home-next-to-lake -3)

--------------------- design32 ---------------------
%-complete rank = 1   Delta rank = 6
The locations of the landuses for design32 are:
(recreational-area lot7)
(apartment-complex lot10)
(housing-sector-1 lot9)
(dumpsite lot5)
The problems for design32 are
(recreational-area unfavorable because-no-lake-nearby 5)
(apartment-complex unfavorable soil-conditions 6)
the opportunities of design32 are
(apartment-complex favorable home-next-to-lake -3)

--------------------- design36 ---------------------
%-complete rank = 1   Delta rank = 6
The locations of the landuses for design36 are:
(recreational-area lot11)
(apartment-complex lot10)
(housing-sector-1 lot9)
(dumpsite lot5)
The problems for design36 are
(recreational-area unfavorable because-no-lake-nearby 5)
(apartment-complex unfavorable soil-conditions 6)
the opportunities of design36 are
(apartment-complex favorable home-next-to-lake -3)

--------------------- design37 ---------------------
%-complete rank = 1   Delta rank = 6
The locations of the landuses for design37 are:
(recreational-area lot7)
(apartment-complex lot12)
(housing-sector-1 lot9)
(dumpsite lot5)
The problems for design37 are
(recreational-area unfavorable because-no-lake-nearby 5)
(apartment-complex unfavorable soil-conditions 6)
the opportunities of design37 are

(apartment-complex favorable home-next-to-lake -3)

--------------------- design41 ---------------------
%-complete rank = 1   Delta rank = 6
The locations of the landuses for design41 are:
(recreational-area lot11)
(apartment-complex lot12)
(housing-sector-1 lot9)
(dumpsite lot5)
The problems for design41 are
(recreational-area unfavorable because-no-lake-nearby 5)
(apartment-complex unfavorable soil-conditions 6)
the opportunities of design41 are
(apartment-complex favorable home-next-to-lake -3)

Please select one
[reject/automatic/continue-search/adapt/redisplay/relax/sort/quit/explore]

Your Selection? ==> reject

> The user decides to reject many designs, even though they
> are pareto optimal. (He feels he cannot handle poor soil conditions.)

Give me a list of nodes you want to reject ==> (design22 design26
design27 design31 design32 design36 design37 design41)

Please select one
[reject/automatic/continue-search/adapt/redisplay/relax/sort/quit/explore]
Your Selection? ==> explore

> The explore command causes a relaxation of 1 to the *delta* and it
> then kicks off the search process. The new *delta* is set to 7.

Setting Delta to 7

**** LOOKING FOR PROBLEMS

Working on: design50
That is nice the apartment-complex can has a view of the lake
The slope at the apartment-complex site is too high.

Working on: design45
I think the cemetery is visible to the high-rising apartment-complex.
The apartment-complex being next to a lake reminds me of my parent 's home.
Bad soil conditions for the apartment-complex has been detected.

Working on: design60
The housing-sector-1 being next to a lake reminds me of my parent 's home.

Bad soil conditions for the housing-sector-1 has been detected.
Oh No The apartment-complex is too close to the ugly highway

Answers found !

Here are some COMPLETE solutions to ponder...

--------------------- design43 ---------------------
%-complete rank = 0   Delta rank = 7
The locations of the landuses for design43 are:
(cemetery lot5)
(recreational-area lot12)
(apartment-complex lot10)
(housing-sector-1 lot9)
(dumpsite lot3)
The problems for design43 are
(apartment-complex unfavorable soil-conditions 6)
(apartment-complex unfavorable cemetery-visible 7)
the opportunities of design43 are
(apartment-complex favorable home-next-to-lake -3)

--------------------- design45 ---------------------
%-complete rank = 0   Delta rank = 7
The locations of the landuses for design45 are:
(cemetery lot5)
(recreational-area lot10)
(apartment-complex lot12)
(housing-sector-1 lot9)
(dumpsite lot3)
The problems for design45 are
(apartment-complex unfavorable soil-conditions 6)
(apartment-complex unfavorable cemetery-visible 7)
the opportunities of design45 are
(apartment-complex favorable home-next-to-lake -3)

--------------------- design46 ---------------------
%-complete rank = 0   Delta rank = 7
The locations of the landuses for design46 are:
(cemetery lot3)
(recreational-area lot12)
(apartment-complex lot10)
(housing-sector-1 lot9)
(dumpsite lot5)
The problems for design46 are
(apartment-complex unfavorable soil-conditions 6)
(apartment-complex unfavorable cemetery-visible 7)
the opportunities of design46 are
(apartment-complex favorable home-next-to-lake -3)

Please Choose any of [reject-accept/redisplay/ignore]
Your response ==> **reject-accept**

Give me a list of nodes you wish to accept ==> <u>0</u>

The user decides to reject all the designs he sees, since he does not want to deal with bad soil conditions.

Are you satisfied with what you have [y/n] ==> <u>n</u>

Give me a list of nodes you wish to reject ==> <u>(design43 design45 design46)</u>

The best delta value is: <u>3</u>
This is value is liable to reduce/increase as we go along

Here are partial/complete solutions to consider:

--------------------- design51 ---------------------
%-complete rank = 1   Delta rank = 3
The locations of the landuses for design51 are:
(recreational-area lot10)
(apartment-complex lot11)
(housing-sector-1 lot9)
(dumpsite lot3)
The problems for design51 are
(apartment-complex unfavorable power-lines-in-view 4)
(apartment-complex unfavorable slope 6)
the opportunities of design51 are
(apartment-complex favorable lake-visible -5)

--------------------- design52 ---------------------
%-complete rank = 1   Delta rank = 3
The locations of the landuses for design52 are:
(recreational-area lot12)
(apartment-complex lot11)
(housing-sector-1 lot9)
(dumpsite lot3)
The problems for design52 are
(apartment-complex unfavorable power-lines-in-view 4)
(apartment-complex unfavorable slope 6)
the opportunities of design52 are
(apartment-complex favorable lake-visible -5)

--------------------- design56 ---------------------
%-complete rank = 1   Delta rank = 3
The locations of the landuses for design56 are:
(recreational-area lot10)
(apartment-complex lot11)
(housing-sector-1 lot9)
(dumpsite lot5)
The problems for design56 are
(apartment-complex unfavorable power-lines-in-view 4)
(apartment-complex unfavorable slope 6)
the opportunities of design56 are

(apartment-complex favorable lake-visible -5)

--------------------- design57 ---------------------
%-complete rank = 1   Delta rank = 3
The locations of the landuses for design57 are:
(recreational-area lot12)
(apartment-complex lot11)
(housing-sector-1 lot9)
(dumpsite lot5)
The problems for design57 are
(apartment-complex unfavorable power-lines-in-view 4)
(apartment-complex unfavorable slope 6)
the opportunities of design57 are
(apartment-complex favorable lake-visible -5)

Please select one
[reject/automatic/continue-search/adapt/redisplay/relax/sort/quit/explore]
 Your Selection? ==> **adapt**

> The user decides to try adapting design57. This choice is currently left
> in the user's hands because it is a very slow process. Under utopian
> conditions, the system should try to adapt every design!

Which one would you like to try adapt? [node#] ==> **design57**

Cleaning up junk nodes, if any..

Here are partial/complete solutions to consider:
> The adapted partial design

--------------------- design83 ---------------------
%-complete rank = 1   Delta rank = -5
The locations of the landuses for design83 are:
(recreational-area lot12)
(apartment-complex lot11)
(housing-sector-1 lot9)
(dumpsite lot5)
the opportunities of design83 are
(apartment-complex favorable lake-visible -5)
The adaptations of design83 are
(apartment-complex action (on building stilts))
(apartment-complex action
                (camouflage the
                        power-lines
                        with
                        green
                        paint
                        and
                        plant-matter))

--------------------- design51 ---------------------
%-complete rank = 1   Delta rank = 3
The locations of the landuses for design51 are:
(recreational-area lot10)
(apartment-complex lot11)
(housing-sector-1 lot9)
(dumpsite lot3)
The problems for design51 are
(apartment-complex unfavorable power-lines-in-view 4)
(apartment-complex unfavorable slope 6)
the opportunities of design51 are
(apartment-complex favorable lake-visible -5)

--------------------- design52 ---------------------
%-complete rank = 1   Delta rank = 3
The locations of the landuses for design52 are:
(recreational-area lot12)
(apartment-complex lot11)
(housing-sector-1 lot9)
(dumpsite lot3)
The problems for design52 are
(apartment-complex unfavorable power-lines-in-view 4)
(apartment-complex unfavorable slope 6)
the opportunities of design52 are
(apartment-complex favorable lake-visible -5)

--------------------- design56 ---------------------
%-complete rank = 1   Delta rank = 3
The locations of the landuses for design56 are:
(recreational-area lot10)
(apartment-complex lot11)
(housing-sector-1 lot9)
(dumpsite lot5)
The problems for design56 are
(apartment-complex unfavorable power-lines-in-view 4)
(apartment-complex unfavorable slope 6)
the opportunities of design56 are
(apartment-complex favorable lake-visible -5)

Please select one:
[reject/automatic/continue-search/adapt/redisplay/relax/sort/quit/explore]

Selection? ==> **continue-search**

> The user decides to continue searching. The system asks for the user's
> preference, if any. The user can either give a node number or just state that
> he is indifferent about choosing among the parto-optimal partial designs.

Choose a node for that you like [node#/indifferent] ==> **design83**
The selection is : design83

Looking for Problems

.... extra output edited out ....

Working on: design86
That is nice the apartment-complex can has a view of the lake

The best delta value is: -6
This is value is liable to reduce/increase as we go along

Answers found !
-------------------- design86 --------------------
%-complete rank = 0   Delta rank = -6
The locations of the landuses for design86 are:
(cemetery lot3)
(recreational-area lot12)
(apartment-complex lot11)
(housing-sector-1 lot9)
(dumpsite lot5)
the opportunities of design86 are
(apartment-complex favorable lake-visible -5)
The adaptations of design86 are
(apartment-complex action
             (camouflage the
                     power-lines
                     with
                     green
                     paint
                     and
                     plant-matter))
(apartment-complex action (on building stilts))

Please Choose any of [reject-accept/redisplay/ignore]
Your response ==> **reject-accept**

Give me a list of nodes you wish to accept ==> **(design86)**

The user has made a selection. He will now try to see if
he can find anything better. If not, he will stop.

Are you satisfied with what you have [y/n] ==> **n**

Give me a list of nodes you wish to reject ==> **nil**

Please select one:
[reject/automatic/continue-search/adapt/redisplay/relax/sort/quit/explore]

Your Selection? ==> **relax**

By how much [#] ==> **5**

---------------------- design51 ----------------------
%-complete rank = 1   Delta rank = 3
The locations of the landuses for design51 are:
(recreational-area lot10)
(apartment-complex lot11)
(housing-sector-1 lot9)
(dumpsite lot3)
The problems for design51 are
(apartment-complex unfavorable power-lines-in-view 4)
(apartment-complex unfavorable slope 6)
the opportunities of design51 are
(apartment-complex favorable lake-visible -5)

---------------------- design52 ----------------------
%-complete rank = 1   Delta rank = 3
The locations of the landuses for design52 are:
(recreational-area lot12)
(apartment-complex lot11)
(housing-sector-1 lot9)
(dumpsite lot3)
The problems for design52 are
(apartment-complex unfavorable power-lines-in-view 4)
(apartment-complex unfavorable slope 6)
the opportunities of design52 are
(apartment-complex favorable lake-visible -5)

---------------------- design56 ----------------------
%-complete rank = 1   Delta rank = 3
The locations of the landuses for design56 are:
(recreational-area lot10)
(apartment-complex lot11)
(housing-sector-1 lot9)
(dumpsite lot5)
The problems for design56 are
(apartment-complex unfavorable power-lines-in-view 4)
(apartment-complex unfavorable slope 6)
the opportunities of design56 are
(apartment-complex favorable lake-visible -5)

Please select one:
[reject/automatic/continue-search/adapt/redisplay/relax/sort/quit/explore]

Your Selection? ==> quit

```
The user is satisfied with what he selected on the previous page.
He decides to stop.
```

=> (exit)

hera<17> logout

References

[Barrow & Tenenbaum 76]
>   Barrow H.G., J.M. Tannenbaum.
>   *MYSYS: A system for reasoning about scenes.*
>   Technical Report TR-121, SRI International, March,
>   1976.

[Brown & Chandrasekaran 86]
>   Brown D.C., B. Chandrasekaran.
>   Expert Systems for a class of Mechanical Design
>   Activity.
>   In Sriram D., Adey B. (editor), *Proceedings of the
>   First International Conference on AI
>   applications in Engineering.* Computational
>   Mechanics, U.K., 1986.

[Buchanan & Feigenbaum 78]
>   Buchanan, B.G., E.A. Fiegenbaum.
>   Dendral and Meta-Dendral: Their Applications
>   Dimension.
>   *Artificial Intelligence* 11(1):5-24, 1978.

[Burstall 69]   Burstall, R.M.
>   A program for solving word sum puzzles.
>   *Computer Journal* 12:48-51, 1969.

[Bushnell & Director 86]
>   Bushnell, M.L., S.W. Director.
>   VLSI CAD Tool Integration Using the Ulysses
>   Environment.
>   In *Proceedings of the 23rd ACM/IEEE Design
>   Automation Conference Proceedings*, pages
>   55-61. 1986.

[Cagan 88]   Cagan, J. and Agogino, A. M.
>   1stPRINCE: Innovative Design from First
>   Principles.
>   In *7th National Conference on Artificial Intelligence.*
>   AAAI-88, Minneapolis, MN, August 21-26,
>   1988.

[Carbonell 83]   Carbonell, J. G.
                    Derivational Analogy and its role in Problem
                        Solving.
                    In *Proceedings AAAI-83, Pittsburgh, PA*, pages
                        64-69. 1983.

[Carbonell 86]   Carbonell, J. G.
                    Derivational Analogy: A Theory of Reconstructive
                        Problem Solving and Expertise Acquisition.
                    In Michalski, R. S., J. G. Carbonell, T. M. Mitchell
                        (editor), *Machine Learning: An Artificial
                        Intelligence Approach Vol 2*. Morgan Kaufman,
                        1986.

[Chankong & Haimes 83]
                    Chankong, V., Y.Y. Haimes.
                    *Multiobjective Decision Making: Theory and
                        Methodology*.
                    North-Holland, 1983.

[Cheyayeb 87]   Cheyayeb, F.
                    *A Framework for Engineering Knowledge
                        Representation and Problem Solving*.
                    PhD thesis, Dept. of Civil Engineering, M.I.T.,
                        Cambridge, MA, May, 1987.

[Coyne et.al. 89]   Coyne R.D., M.A. Rosenman, A.D. Radford,
                    M. Balachandaran, J.S. Gero.
                    Knowledge-Based Design Systems.
                    Addison Wesley, 1989.

[Darwin 59]   Darwin, C.
                    *On the Origin of Species by Means of Natural
                        Selection*.
                    London: John Murray, 1859.

[Deutsch 66]   Deutsch, J.P.A., J.P.A. Deutsch.
                    A short cut for certain combinatorial problems.
                    In *British Joint Computer Conference*. 1966.

[Dyer et.al. 86]   Dyer M.G., M. Flowers, J. Hodges.
                    EDISON: An Engineering Design Invention System
                        Operating Naively.
                    In *Proceedings of the First International Conference
                        on Applicatoins of AI to Engineering*. April,
                        1986.

[Evans 68] Evans, T. G.
A Program for the Solution of a Class of Geometric
Analogy Intelligence Test Questions.
In Minsky, M. (editor), *Semantic Information
Processing*. MIT Press, Cambridge, 1968.

[Feigenbaum 71] Feigenbaum E. A. , Buchanan B. G. and Lederberg
J.
On Generality and Problem Solving: a Case Study
Using the DENDRAL Program.
Machine Intelligence. Volume 6..
Edinburgh University Press, Edinburgh, Scotland,
1971, pages 165-190.

[Fikes 69] Fikes, R. E.
*REF-ARF: A System For Solving Problems Related
as Procedures.*
Technical Report Technical Note 14, Stanford
Research Institute, September, 1969.

[Fikes 70] Fikes, R.E.
A system for solving problems stated as procedures.
Artificial Intelligence 1:27-120, 1970.

[Fox 83] Fox, M.S.
*Constraint Directed Search: A case of Job Shop
Scheduling.*
PhD thesis, Carnegie-Mellon University, 1983.

[Gentner 83] Gentner, D.
Structure Mapping: A Theoretical Framework for
Analogy.
Cognitive Science 7, 1983.

[Gentner & Toupin 86]
Gentner, D., C. Toupin.
Systematicity and Surface Similarity in the
Development of Analogy.
Cognitive Science 10:277-300, 1986.

[Gero 87] Gero, J.S.
*Prototypes: a new schema for knowledge-based
design.*
Technical Report, Architectural Computing Unit,
Department of Architectural Science, Working
Paper, 1987.

[Gero et.al. 88]   Gero, J.S., M.L. Maher, W. Zhang.
                     Chunking structural design knowledge and
                          prototypes.
                     In Gero, J.S. (editor), *Artificial Intelligence in
                          Engineering: Design*. CMP/Elsevier, 1988.

[Goel 89]   Goel, A.K.
                     *Integration of Case-Based Reasoning and Model-
                          Based Reasoning for Adaptive Design Problem
                          Solving*.
                     PhD thesis, The Ohio State University, 1989.

[Goel & Chandrasekaran 89]
                     Goel, A., B. Chandrasekaran.
                     Functional Representation of Designs and Redisng
                          Problem Solving.
                     In *Proceedings of the Eleventh (IJCAI) International
                          Joint Conference on Artificial Intelligence*, pages
                          1399-1394. 1989.

[Goicoechea 82]   Goicoechea A., D.R. Hansen, L. Duckstein.
                     *Multibobjective Decision Analysis With Engineering
                          and Business Applications*.
                     John Wiley & Sons, 1982.

[Golomb 65]   Golomb, S.W., L.D. Baumert.
                     Backtrack Programming.
                     Journal of the ACM :516-524, 1965.

[Golomb and Baumert 65]
                     Golomb, S.W., L.D. Baumert.
                     Backtrack Programming.
                     J. of the ACM 12, 1965.

[Gordon 61]   Gordon W.J.
                     Synectics: The development of Creative Capacity.
                     Harper & Row, Publishers, NY, 1961.

[Gross 86]   Gross, M.D.
                     Design as Exploring Constraints.
                     PhD thesis, M.I.T., 1986.

[Guilford 59]   Guilford, J.P.
                     Creativity.
                     American Psychologist (5):444-454, 1959.

[Habraken 83]   Habraken, J.N.
                     *Writing Form, the notation of form transformations
                     in a built environment.*
                     Technical Report, M.I.T., Cambridge, MA, August,
                     1983.

[Haimes etal. 75]   Haimes, Y.Y., W.A. Hall, H.T. Freedman.
                     *Multiobjective Optimization in Water Resources
                     Systems: The Surrogate Worth Trade-off (SWT)
                     Method.*
                     Elsevier, Amsterdam, 1975.

[Hammond 86]   Hammond, K.J.
                     CHEF: A Model of Case-based Planning.
                     In *Proceedings of AAAI-86*, pages 267-271. 1986.

[Haralick 80]   Haralick, R.M.
                     Scene matching methods.
                     In Haralick, R.M., J.C. Simon (editor), *Issues in
                     Digital Image Processing*, pages 221-243.
                     Sijthoff and Noordhoff, Alphen aan den Rijn,
                     Netherlands, 1980.

[Haralick and Elliot 80]
                     Haralick R.M., G.L. Elliot.
                     Increasing tree search efficiency for constraint
                     satisfaction problems.
                     Artificial Intelligence 14:263-313, 1980.

[Hart, Nilsson & Raphael 68]
                     Hart, P.E., N.J. Nilsson, and B. Raphael.
                     A formal basis for the heuristic determination of
                     minimum cost paths.
                     *IEEE Transactions on Systems Science and
                     Cybernetics* SSC-4(2):100-107, 1968.

[Huhns 87]   Huhns M.H., R.D. Acosta.
                     *Argo: An Analogical Reasoning System for Solving
                     Design Problems.*
                     Technical Report AI/CAD-092-87, Microelectronic
                     and Computer Technology Corporation, March,
                     1987.

[Kass & Leake 88]
>   Kass, A.M., D.B. Leake.
>   Case-Based Reasoning Applied to Constructing
>   Explanations.
>   In *Proceedings of the DARPA Workshop on Case-
>   based Reasoning*, pages 190-208. May 10-13,
>   1988.

[Kedar-Cabelli 85a]
>   Kedar-Cabelli S. T.
>   Purpose-Directed Analogy.
>   In *Proceedings of the Cognitive Science Society
>   Conference*. August, 1985.

[Kedar-Cabelli 85b]
>   Kedar-Cabelli, S.T.
>   *Analogy - From a unified perspective*.
>   Technical Report ML-TR-3, Department of
>   Computer Science, Rutgers University,
>   December, 1985.

[Kedar-Cabelli 85c]
>   Kedar-Cabelli, S.T.
>   Purpose-Directed Analogy.
>   In *Proceedings of the Cognitive Science Society
>   Conference*. Irvine, CA, August, 1985.

[Kolodner 80]   Kolodner, J.L.
>   *Retrieval and organizational strategies in
>   conceptual memory: A computer model*.
>   PhD thesis, Yale University, 1980.

[Kolodner 81]   Kolodner, J.L.
>   Organization and retrieval in a conceptual memory
>   for events.
>   In *Proceedings of the Seventh International Joint
>   Conference on Artificial Intelligence*. 1981.

[Kolodner 85]   Kolodner, J. L., Simpson, R. L. Jr., Sycara-
>   Cyransky, K.
>   A Process Model of Case-Based Reasoning in
>   Problem-Solving.
>   In *Proceedings IJCAI-9*. Los Angeles, CA, August,
>   1985.

[Kolodner 87]   Kolodner, J.L.
                  Extending Problem Solver Capabilities Through
                      Case-Based Inference.
                  In *Proceedings of the Machine Learning Workshop*.
                      June, 1987.

[Korf 85]   Korf, R.K.
                  Depth-First Iterative-Deepening: An Optimal
                      Admissible Tree Search.
                  Int. J. of Artificial Intelligence 27(1):97-109, 1985.

[Kuhn 70]   Kuhn, T.S.
                  The structure of scientific revolutions.
                  University of Chicago Press, 1970.

[Langley et.al. 87] Langley, P., H.A. Simon, G.L. Bradshaw, J.M.
                      Zytkow.
                  *Scientific Discovery - Computational Explorations of
                      the Creative Processes.*
                  The MIT Press, Cambridge, MA, 1987.

[Lenat 76]   Lenat, D.B.
                  *AM: An artificial intelligence approach to discovery
                      in mathematics as heuristic search.*
                  PhD thesis, Stanford University, STAN-CS-76-570,
                      1976.

[Lenat 84]   Lenat, D.B.
                  Why AM and EURISKO Appear to Work.
                  Artificial Intelligence 24:269-294, 1984.

[Lindsay 80]   Lindsay, R., Buchanan, B., Feigenbaum, E. and
                      Lederberg, J.
                  *Applications of Artificial Intelligence for Chemical
                      Inference : The Dendral Project.*
                  McGraw-Hill Book Company, 1980.

[Mackworth 77]   Mackworth A.K.
                  Consistency in networks of relations.
                  Artificial Intelligence 8:99-118, 1977.

[Maher 84]   Maher, M. L.
                  HI-RISE: An Expert System For The Preliminary
                      Structural Design Of High Rise Buildings.
                  PhD thesis, Dept. Civil Engineering, Carnegie-
                      Mellon University, 1984.

[McDonnell Douglas 84]
                  McDonnell Douglas Corporation.
                  Graphic Design System.
                  1984

[McLaughlin and Gero 87]
                  McLaughlin, S., J.S. Gero.
                  Acquiring expert knwoledge from characterized
                      designs.
                  Artificial Intelligence for Engineering Design,
                      Analysis and Manufacturing 1(2):73-87, 1987.

[Minsky 75]   Minsky, M.
                  A framework for representing knowledge.
                  In Winston P.H. (editor), *The Psychology of*
                      Computer Vision. McGraw-Hill, New York,
                      1975.

[Mittal 85]   Mittal, S., Dym, C. and Morjaria, M.
                  PRIDE: An Expert System for the Design of Paper
                      Handling Systems.
                  In Dym, C. (editor), *Applications of Knowledge-*
                      Based Systems to Engineering Analysis and
                      Design, pages 99-116. American Society of
                      Mechanical Engineers, 1985.

[Mostow 85]   Mostow, J.
                  Toward Better Models Of The Design Process.
                  The AI Magazine , Spring, 1985.

[Muller 87]   Muller, E.T.
                  Daydreaming and Computation: A Computer Model
                      of Everyday Creativity, Learning, and Emotions
                      in the Human Stream of Thought.
                  PhD thesis, Univ. of California, Los Angeles,
                      UCLA-AI-87-8, February, 1987.

[Murthy & Addanki 87]
                  Murthy, S.S., S. Addanki.
                  PROMPT: An Innovative Design Tool.
                  In *Proceedings of the sixth national conference on*
                      artificial intelligence, pages 637-642. 1987.

[Nadel 85a]   Nadel, B.A.
                     *The Consistent Labeling Problem: Backround and
                     Problem Formulation.*
                     Technical Report DCS-TR-164, University of
                     Michigan, 1985.

[Nadel 85b]   Nadel, B.A.
                     *The Consistent Labeling Problem: Subproblems,
                     Enumerations and Constraint Satisfiability.*
                     Technical Report DCS-TR-165, University of
                     Michigan, 1985.

[Nadel 85c]   Nadel, B.A.
                     *The Consistent Labeling Problem: The Generalized
                     Backtracking Algorithm.*
                     Technical Report DCS-TR-166, University of
                     Michigan, 1985.

[Nadel 85d]   Nadel, B.A.
                     *The Consistent Labeling Problem: The Generalized
                     Forward Checking and Word-Wise Forward
                     Checking Algorithms.*
                     Technical Report DCS-TR-167, University of
                     Michigan, 1985.

[Navinchandra 85]
                     Navinchandra D.
                     *IMST user's manual: A tool for building Rule-based
                     Expert Systems.*
                     Technical Report CCRE-85-6, Center for
                     Construction Research and Education, M.I.T.,
                     1985.

[Navinchandra 86a]
                     Navinchandra, D. and Marks, D. H.
                     Design Exploration through Constraint Relaxation.
                     In Gero, J. (editor), *Expert Systems in Computer-
                     Aided Design.* North-Holland, 1986.

[Navinchandra 86b]
                     Navinchandra D.
                     *Intelligent Use of Constraints for Activity
                     Scheduling.*
                     Technical Report CERL N-86/15, US Army Corps
                     of Engineers, Construction Engineering Research
                     Laboratory, July, 1986.

[Navinchandra 87]
          Navinchandra, D.
          *Exploring for Innovative Designs by Relaxing
              Criteria and reasoning from Precedent-Based
              Knowledge.*
          PhD thesis, M.I.T., 1987.

[Navinchandra 88]
          Navinchandra, D.
          Case-Based Reasoning in CYCLOPS, a Design
              Problem Solver.
          In Kolodner, J. (editor), *Proceedings of the DARPA
              Workshop on Case-based Reasoning*, pages
              286-301. Morgan Kaufman, 1988.

[Navinchandra 90]
          Navinchandra, D.
          *Innovative Design Systems, Where are we and
              Where do we go from here?.*
          Technical Report CMU-RI-TR-90-01, Robotics
              Institute, Carnegie Mellon University, 1990.

[Navinchandra et.al. 87]
          Navinchandra D., D. Sriram, S.T. Kedar-Cabelli.
          On the Role of Analogy in Engineering Design: An
              Overview.
          In D. Sriram, B. Adey (editor), *AI in Engineering,
              Proceedings of the 2nd Intl. Conference, Boston.*
          Computational Mechanics Publishing, U.K.,
              1987.

[Nijenhius and Wilf 75]
          Nijenhuis, A., H.S. Wilf.
          Combinatorial Algorithms.
          Academic Press, New York, 1975.

[Nillson 71]   Nillson. N. J.
          Problem-Solving Methods in Artificial Intelligence.
          McGraw Hill Book Company, 1971.

[Nilsson 80]   Nilsson, N.J.
          Principles of Artificial Intelligence.
          Tioga, Palo Alto, CA, 1980.

[Osborn 53]   Osborn, A. F.
                   Applied Imagination.
                   Charles Scribner's Sons, New York, 1953.

[Pareto 96]   Pareto, V.
                   Cors d'Economie Politique.
                   Rouge, Lausanne, Switzerland, 1896.

[Pearl 84]   Pearl, J.
                   *Heuristics - Intelligent search strategies for
                       computer problem solving.*
                   Addison Wesley, Reading, MA, 1984.

[Pfefferkorn 75]   Pfefferkorn, C.E.
                   The Design Problem Solver: A System for
                       Designing Equipment or Furniture Layouts.
                   In Eastman, C.M. (editor), *Spatial Synthesis in
                       Computer-Aided Building Design.* , 1975.

[Radford & Gero 86]
                   Radford, A.D., J.S. Gero.
                   Multicriteria Optimization in Architectural Design.
                   In Gero, J.S. (editor), *Design Optimization.*
                   Academic Press, Inc., New York, NY, 1986.

[Rickards 74]   Rickards, T.
                   Problem Solving through Creative Analysis.
                   Wiley, NY, 1974.

[Roos 66]   Roos, D.
                   ICES System Design.
                   MIT Press, Cambridge, MA., 1966.

[Rychner et.al. 86]Rychner, M.D., Farinacci, M.L., Hulthage, I., Fox,
                   M.S.
                   *Integration of Multiple Knowledge Sources in
                       ALADIN, an Alloy Design System.*
                   Technical Report, Intelligent Systems Laboratory,
                       Robotics Institute, Carnegie-Mellon University,
                       1986.

[Schank 77]   Schank, R. C. And Abelson, R.
                   Scripts, Plans, Goals, and Understanding.
                   Erlbaum, Hillsdale, N.J., 1977.

[Schank 82]   Schank, R.C.
                   *Dynamic Memory: A Theory of reminding and
                       learning in computers and people.*
                   Cambridge University Press, 1982.

[Schank 86]   Schank, R.C.
                   *Explanation Patterns: Understanding Mechanically
                       and Creatively.*
                   Lawrence Erlbaum Associates, Hillsdale, NJ, 1986.

[Schank 88]   Schank, R.
                   *The Creative Attitude: Learning to ask and answer
                       the right questions.*
                   Erlbaum, 1988.

[Simmons 88]   Simmons, R.
                   *Combining Associational and Causal Reasoning to
                       Solve Interpretation and Planning Problems.*
                   PhD thesis, M.I.T., 1988.

[Soukup 81]   Soukup, J.
                   Circuit Layout.
                   Proceedings of the IEEE 69(10), Oct, 1981.

[SPICE2 75]   SPICE Group.
                   *SPICE2, A computer program to simulate
                       semiconductor circuits.*
                   Technical Report ERL-M520, University of
                       California Berkeley, 1975.

[Sriram 86]   Sriram, D.
                   *Knowledge-Based Approaches for Structural
                       Design.*
                   PhD thesis, Carnegie Mellon University, 1986.

[Stallman & Sussman 77]
                   Stallman, R., G.J. Sussman.
                   Forward Reasoning and Dependency Directed
                       Backtracking in a system for computer aided
                       circuit analysis.
                   Artificial Intelligence 9:135-196, 1977.

[Stefik 80]   Stefik, M.
                   Planning with Constraints.
                   PhD thesis, Stanford University, STAN-CS-80-784,
                       1980.

[Steinberg 87]   Steinberg, L.I.
                   Design as Refinement Plus Constraint Propagation:
                       The VEXED Experience.
                   In *Proceedings of the sixth national conference on
                       Artificial Intelligence*, pages 830-835. 1987.

[Steinberg et.al. 86]
                   Steinberg L., N. Langrana, T. Mitchell, J. Mostow,
                   C. Tong.
                   *A Domain Independent Model of Knowledge-Based
                       Design.*
                   Technical Report AI/VLSI Project Working Paper
                       No. 33, Rutgers Universtiy, March, 1986.

[Tomlin 86]   Tomlin, D. Professor, Graduate School or Design,
                   Harvard University.
                   1986
                   Personal Communication.

[Tong 86]   Tong, C.
                   *A framework for organizing and evaluating
                       knowledge-based models of the design process.*
                   Technical Report AI/VLSI Project Working Paper
                       No. 21, Rutgers University, 1986.

[Tong 88]   Tong, C.
                   Knowledge-Based Circuit Design.
                   PhD thesis, Stanford University, 1988.

[Tversky 77]   Tversky, A.
                   Features of Similarity.
                   Psychology Review 84(4), July, 1977.

[Ullman & Dietterich 87]
                   Ullman, D.G., T.A. Dietterich.
                   Mechanical Design Methodology: Implications on
                       Future Developments of Computer-Aided Design
                       and Knowledge-Based Systems.
                   Engineering with Computers 2:21-29, 1987.

[Walker 60]   Walker, R.J.
                   An enumerative technique for a class of
                       combinatorial problems.
                   In *Combinatorial Analysis (Proc. Symp. Applied
                       Math., Vol X), American Mathematical Society*.
                       1960.

[Waltz 75]   Waltz, D.
                   Understanding line drawings of scenes with
                       shadows.
                   In Winston P.H. (editor), *The Psychology of
                       Computer Vision*. McGraw-Hill New York,
                       1975.

[Wilde 78]   Wilde, D. J.
                   .]: *Globally Optimal Design*.
                   Wiley, New York, 1978.

[Winston 80]   Winston, P. H.
                   Learning and Reasonig by Analogy.
                   Communications of the ACM 23(12), December,
                       1980.

[Winston 81]   Winston, P. H.
                   *Learning New Principles from Precedents and
                       Exercises: The Details*.
                   Technical Report AI Lab Memo 632, MIT, A.I. Lab,
                       1981.

[Winston et.al. 83]
                   Winston, P. H., T.O. Binford, B. Katz, M. Lowry.
                   Learning Physical Descriptions from Functional
                       Definitions, Examples and Precedents.
                   In *Proceedings of AAAI-83*. August, 1983.

[Zionts 77]   Zionts, S.
                   Integer linear programming with multiple objectives.
                   Annals of Discrete Mathematics :551-562, 1977.

[Zionts & Wallenius 80]
                   Zionts, S., J. Wallenius.
                   Identifying efficient vectors: some theory and
                       computational results.
                   Operations Research 24:785-793, 1980.

Index

Springer Series
SYMBOLIC COMPUTATION - *Artificial Intelligence (continued)*

L. Bolc, M.J. Coombs (Eds): *Expert System Applications.* IX, 471 pages, 84 figs., 1988.

C.-H. Tzeng: *A Theory of Heuristic Information in Game-Tree Search.* X, 107 pages, 22 figs., 1988.

H. Coelho, J.C. Cotta: *Prolog by Example. How to Learn, Teach, and Use It.* X, 382 pages, 68 figs., 1988.

L. Kanal, V. Kumar (Eds): *Search in Artificial Intelligence.* X, 482 pages, 67 figs., 1988.

H. Abramson, V. Dahl: *Logic Grammars.* XIV, 234 pages, 40 figs., 1989.

R. Hausser: *Computation of Language. An Essay on Syntax, Semantics, and Pragmatics in Natural Man-Machine Communication.* XVI, 425 pages, 1989.

B. D'Ambrosio: *Qualitative Process Theory Using Linguistic Variables.* X, 156 pages, 22 figs., 1989.

A. Kobsa, W. Wahlster (Eds): *User Models in Dialog Systems.* IX, 471 pages, 113 figs., 1989.

P. Besnard: *An introduction to Default Logic.* XI, 208 pages, 1989.

V. Kumar. P.S. Gopalakrishnan, L. Kanal (Eds): *Parallel Algorithms for Machine Intelligence and Vision.* XII, 433 pages, 148 figs., 1990.

Y. Peng, J.A. Reggia: *Abductive Interference Models for Diagnostic Problem-Solving.* XI, 304 pages, 25 figs., 1990.

D. Navinchandra: *Exploration and Innovation in Design.* XI, 196 pages, 51 figs., 1991.